EMOTIONAL CLEANSING

EMOTIONAL CLEANSING

The Spiritual Journey
Toward A
Clear Heart

Marty Klein

Creative Arts Book Company
Berkeley ∾ California

Emotional Cleansing
is published by Donald S. Ellis
and distributed by Creative Arts Book Company

For information contact:
Creative Arts Book Company
833 Bancroft Way
Berkeley, California 94710
(800) 848-7789

ISBN 0-88739-347-0
Library of Congress Catalog Number 00-103035

Printed in the United States of America

Acknowledgments

Many thanks go out to the people who directly and indirectly helped me with this book. Thanks to all those named below and to all the people who are not listed who know they had a part in helping me learn about our human condition.

Thanks to Don Ellis and Creative Arts Book Company for having faith in me and this book. Thanks to the editors, Cassia Berman, Perdita Finn, Laura Newton, Paul Samuelson, and Terry Pride. Thanks for hanging in there with me and teaching me more about English than I ever wanted to know.

Thanks to Harvey Jackins, Charlie Kreiner and all my associates in the Reevaluation Counseling community who helped me understand the difference between my inherent goodness and my acquired distressess.

Thanks to Tam Cooper, Alan Sachs, Ellie Kramer, Liz Friedman, Bruce Margolis, Jonathan Kliger, September Heart, Cindy Dern, Judith Simon, and all my Woodstock friends who have shared their lives, their thoughts, and their feelings with me throughout the years. The essence of this book comes from the time I spent with all of you in Woodstock.

Thanks to Marcy Tracy, Henry Hall, Debo Powers, Lora Silvanima, Norine Cardia, Ian Granick, Ken Ross, Patience Gaia, Heidi Fox, Irwin Friedman, Tamara Weinstein, Susie Howell, Kaity Power, Douglas Whitehouse, Cat Keen, Barry Fraser, Walter Thomas, Terry Schneider, and so many other friends and acquaintances for opening up your arms and hearts and warmly welcoming me into the Tallahassee community. Your love and support has been instrumental in providing a stable home environment as I completed the final touches on this book.

ᴔᴔᴔ

To Gretchen, my partner, my lover, and my best friend, and to Milly, a beautiful spirit and a constant source of joy in my life.

෴

CONTENTS

Introduction / 1

PART 1: The Toxins / 9
Chapter 1: Self-Criticism / 11
Chapter 2: Greed / 23
Chapter 3: Jealousy / 31
Chapter 4: Depression / 37
Chapter 5: Abuse / 43
Chapter 6: Guilt / 51
Chapter 7: Worry / 57
Chapter 8: Blame / 63
Chapter 9: Pretense / 69
Chapter 10: Addictions / 75
Chapter 11: Powerlessness / 81

PART 2: The Cleansers / 89
Chapter 1: Tears / 91
Chapter 2: Trembling / 99
Chapter 3: Raging / 107
Chapter 4: Laughter / 113
Chapter 5: Touch / 119
Chapter 6: Help / 125
Chapter 7: Subtle Hidden Cleansers / 131

PART 3: Toward a Clear Heart / 143
Chapter 1: Courage / 145
Chapter 2: Commitment / 149
Chapter 3: Trust / 153
Chapter 4: Integrity / 157

∿∿∿

EMOTIONAL CLEANSING

Introduction
꩜ ꩜ ꩜

The other morning I woke up from a lousy night of sleep. I was groggy, pissed off, and frankly not in good shape at all. A good friend was coming over shortly to visit. She was going through a hard time in her life, and I really wanted to be available with compassion and support.

I went outside, took a few deep breaths, and checked in with myself. "What do I need?" I thought. I scanned my body and got in touch with all the physical sensations I was feeling from head to toe. "Hmmm...a little achy and a whole lot blocked." I then scanned my mind, noticing what thoughts were in my internal dialogue. "Negative recordings bouncing around at random," I soberly admitted to myself. I quickly assessed the situation and then decided what I thought would be the best course of action. I asked my partner Gretchen if she would go for a walk with me and listen to me some. I thought that moving would be good for my body. I needed to move the energy that had gotten blocked from the restless night of sleep. Getting some attention would be good for my mind, I thought; some relaxed attention from another human being, so I could do a little mental rearranging and emotional cleansing.

We went for a hearty three-mile walk and, with Gretchen's loving attention, I complained a little about my lousy night of sleep, cried a little about some things I felt upset about, laughed a little, and made some good decisions about the rest of the day.

About an hour later we returned and I was in a completely different frame of mind. The energy had shifted in my body and my attitude had shifted as well. It felt great to know that I now, as a fifty -year-old man, had the sensitivity to listen to my body and mind, be aware enough to actually understand my body, and then to have my life set up in a way that, most of the time, I can get what I need to function well. I thought back, flashing on all the years I struggled as a younger man. I sadly remembered how I was once deeply disconnected from my physical body and my emotions, and how I unconsciously acted out so many painful drama scenes with no clue of how to help myself.

Most men and women have been clobbered with this kind of conditioning that methodically disconnects them from their emotions, leading to numbness and confusion. We, as human beings, have four bodies to pay attention to and nurture: the spiritual body, the mental body, the physical body, and the emotional body. All four seem to be crucial for a deeply connected life.

We have lots of places in our society to develop our spiritual body—our churches, synagogues and mosques. Safety to worship, whatever our chosen faith, is respected and supported by the law in our country. We are encouraged to develop our mental body in schools, colleges, universities, and other institutions of higher learning. Getting an education is encouraged for all of our citizens, required for all of our children.

We are encouraged to develop our physical bodies through

sports, organized athletics of all kinds, gyms, health spas, and fitness centers. The well-conditioned athlete is cheered and emulated by the youth in our society. Good nutrition has increased in our society, with a growing number of people concerned about living longer and staying in good physical shape. This is all very good—as far as it goes.

As a society, however, we've been totally lacking in support and encouragement for the development of the emotional body. Most of the time we're even discouraged from showing our feelings, with the hidden fear of being identified as crazy for showing too much emotion, and with the ultimate threat of being carted away to a mental institution if we don't comply with the norm and "keep our feelings more together" and "under control." Boys are trained to suppress feelings in general, and especially their grief and fear, almost as a rite of passage toward manhood. Women have been trained to believe that they are weaker because they show more emotions than men, but they are also taught that it's not very feminine to express any form of anger.

I, along with everybody else, was born with a wonderful and healthy emotional body. However, not only was society encouraging me to ignore my feelings, but my childhood experiences reinforced that cultural conditioning. My father beat me often and regularly terrorized me, forcing me to submit to all of his demands. He intimidated the whole family, but only hit me. My mother was always worrying about my health and well being, and with good reason, but was incapable of redirecting my father's rage. I remember constantly feeling terrified and being in lots of pain. I cried and trembled a lot, but the onslaught continued.

At some point in my early training I unconsciously made a decision to numb out rather than continue to feel. The emotional as well as physical pain I was experiencing was too great for me to handle, and there was nobody around to give me support. I, along with millions of others who found themselves in similar situations, made this decision, with or without awareness, as a creative solution to an impossible situation. This choice to stop feeling also inhibited the body's healing process. Although this decision and subsequent behavior may have been useful at the time, they ultimately dealt a devastating blow to our ability to experience our full humanity.

Years later, when I was almost thirty and had gone through the devastating blow of physically losing my sight, I embarked on an incredibly interesting healing journey. I had lost my vision completely but was still very much alive. This loss of sight brought me face to face with the reality that my whole existence was not guaranteed. It was at that moment I realized how precious it was to be alive and how I still could have a full and meaningful existence—if I could stop the destructive behavior that I developed as a result of my painful childhood.

After dabbling in a few different types of therapies, I got involved in Re-Evaluation Counseling with an international community of people who were similarly working toward healing their own emotional bodies. Together we learned skills that helped us cleanse our bodies and minds of the negative baggage we were all carrying. We also learned how to be supportive of each other, developing the ability to assist each other in our healing.

I started to understand, on an intellectual as well as emotional level, how old painful events from the past could cause irrational functioning in the present. This was all great stuff, something that every person on the planet should know. I didn't understand why we had never learned this in school, but I was thrilled and delighted that I had discovered it for myself. I became passionate about learning. I ordered journals and cassettes, counseled a few times a week, went to workshops as much as I could, and immersed myself in the healing process.

Reclaiming my body's healing process, allowing my body to heal itself, has been a truly enlightening adventure for me over the past twenty years. I plan to continue down this path for the rest of my life. I love feeling alive everyday, whether I experience pain or pleasure. I know what to do with my waves of emotions and I hardly ever have that old numbness anymore. Numbed-out people carry a heaviness, a hopelessness about ever getting help for anything, and have a tendency to act like they don't need anything from anybody. It's very difficult for them to trust in others. They lost the ability to trust at a very young age when they showed their emotions and got punished or abandoned, and subsequently were left to deal with life and its complexities on their own.

Thawing out the human from years of numbness is challenging. But the good news is that all human beings are still intact on some deep level, with their full humanity, waiting to thaw out from the deep freeze. Of course, the degree of numbness that we carry is directly proportional to the amount of emotional freedom we were allowed or denied as children.

Reclaiming one's ability to feel emotions is a crucial part of the cleansing process. But it is very much like driving a car—just because you found the key and figured out how to start the car, does not mean that you know how to drive. There's a lot to learn. The world of emotions is filled with untold richness, but it is also filled with many traps, storms, and beds of quicksand. Not only do we need to learn how to keep our emotional vehicles on the proper path, protecting ourselves from others who are driving recklessly, but each of us needs to methodically develop our own emotional infrastructure—bridges, tunnels, roads, and shelters that will safely transport us from one emotional place to another.

For most of us there is a buildup over the years of emotional toxins from a combination of cultural and personal childhood experiences. We need to go through a process of not just talking about, identifying, and analyzing those toxins, but actually cleansing them from our bodies and eventually reaching a place of emotional calmness and mental clarity.

Over the years I have seen so many good people, clients and counselors alike, become so totally infatuated with expressing their emotions and obsessed with the process of releasing emotional toxins, that they lose sight of the reason they are doing the releasing. Obsession with emotional releasing and cleaning up distresses can be equally as destructive as numbness and denial!

I've observed many people who attempt to seek out and eliminate every little piece of distress before feeling good enough about themselves to enjoy life. This is a perfect example of how the medicine or cure can easily become an addiction. The growing preoccupation with distress can often lead people to states of disease and paranoia. This is not loving to one's self. The following symbolic story exemplifies a balanced state of health and well-being. Each one of us has the potential to achieve this in our lives.

A gardener spent the day pulling weeds, readying the soil, and then planting seeds for the spring garden. After the day's work, she came in to clean up. Her hands and arms were dirty and her face was glistening with sweat from hours of hard work. Without much thought, she grabbed the soap, turned the water on, and began washing. The water felt good on her skin as she cleaned. The soap did a good job of cleansing her hands, arms, and face of the sweat, dirt, and grime that had accumulated from the day of work. She rinsed off, briefly scanned her now-clean body, dried off, and left the room.

Emotional cleansing is very similar to cleansing the body of sweat and dirt from a day's work. The only difference is we are cleaning the emotional body. When we've worked through all the inhibitions or compulsions, pretenses, denials, or neurotic obsessions acquired from our earlier training, then the cleansing of the emotional body can become second nature.

The gardener did not go to the sink, talk to herself about the importance of washing, stare at the soap, and procrastinate while the water kept running. That would have been just like so many people in our society who talk about their feelings but don't actually feel them.

The gardener did not wash over and over again, for hours and hours, just to make sure that she got every speck of bacteria off her body. Many people who are in touch with their emotions get lost in obsessing about their distress, desperately wanting to clean it and clean it and clean it...

Emotional cleansing leads to emotional clarity. When we reclaim our ability to feel our emotions and develop the ability to release any buildup of emotional tension, we will then be in a position to function in the world with clear hearts, allowing our love to freely flow.

Each one of us has a gardener in our core waiting patiently to be set free, but eager to get back to the garden. And when we each begin to reclaim our inner gardener and discover our own unique path back to the garden, then we will experience a deep connection to our spiritual nature. Thus the journey of emotional cleansing, leading us toward a clear heart, is also the journey toward our spirituality.

PART 1: The Toxins

✿✿✿

Throughout this book I talk about a crucial concept I call "Emotional Toxins." I discuss in detail the negative effects that these toxins have on our bodies and our lives, and then give an in-depth explanation of the importance of releasing emotional toxins as a key step in permanent healing.

There are two types of emotional toxins. The first type is the accumulated emotional tension that has gradually built up from years of stressful situations, including physical traumas, mental confusion, and emotional obsessions and inhibitions. This stored-up tension methodically distorts our thinking and our view of the world; places a burden on our natural enthusiasm for life; and disconnects us from our bodies, other humans, and our planet. The toxins are like microscopic particles of dust that stick to a window. You can't see them at first but, in time, your ability to see out the window diminishes until your vision is obscured completely.

The second type of emotional toxin has to do with the effects of this distorted vision of life. We develop a strong tendency in our society to compulsively go after things that can only bring us more pain, more disconnection, and more isolation in the long run. These toxins will be exposed and examined in depth in the following chapters of Part 1.

Emotional toxins are not emotions. They are the result of the constant inhibition and distortion of the natural release of emotions. The releasing of emotional toxins is a part of our natural healing process and it tends often to take place as a result of trust and the letting go of some form of control.

As children we all were open and trusting until we got hurt. With inadequate emotional release and confusing misinformation, sometimes innocently given to us by those who cared for us, we unconsciously began to trust less and less. The less we trusted in life and people, the more we desired control over daily events and relationships. Vulnerability was avoided, while control slowly became a compulsive desire in many of us. Unfortunately, irrational control, once achieved, is very difficult to voluntarily suspend.

The desire to control, and for that matter to be controlled, is deeply entrenched in all of the toxins you will read about in the following chapters. The emotional and spiritual growth you wish for can only be attained if you are willing to responsibly suspend these patterns of control.

CHAPTER 1: SELF-CRITICISM

Do you think that no matter what you do, it's just not good enough? Do you think you're not as smart as you should be? Do you think you're not strong enough, not playful enough, not assertive enough, not attractive enough, not sexy enough, not kind enough, not ambitious enough, or not tough enough? Or do you think those thoughts about other people in your life? Do you find that the closer you get to people, the more pathetic they seem? On the other hand, do you think the reverse—that the closer you get to others, the more pathetic you will appear to them? Does your critical pattern focus on the excesses? Are you too much, too intense, too pushy, too wild and crazy, too promiscuous? As a mirror, do you see others as too much?

It seems like everybody has a critical pattern. The pattern can either focus on the outside world or can be aimed internally at ourselves. When the pattern is active, it notices everything and immediately makes a judgment about what it sees. This is based on some distorted value system that has a rigid and very narrow idea of perfection. If it's focused on the external world, the pattern, dressed in attitudes of arrogance, condemnation, repulsion, or hostility, points out all the imperfections of people, places, or things. If the pattern is focused internally, the person with the pattern tends to be especially critical of him or herself, invalidating everything from A to Z. The pattern's whole existence is to criticize, so there is no room at all for even the slightest positive thought. There is only room within the pattern to point out where we are "not enough" or "too much."

A while back, I was eating lunch with a good friend at a local restaurant in the town of Woodstock. The conversation we were having shifted to a discussion about critical people. Hilary began to talk about her mother, describing how her mom was always criticizing something or someone. Hilary was trying to be light and playful, but the thought of her mother's constant criticism was clearly weighing her down.

Just then, a woman in a booth on the other side of the restaurant began to choke on a bite of food. The woman kept choking, but nobody went to her aid. It was lunchtime and the restaurant was packed, but not one person had the clarity of mind to help the woman.

Hilary ran over to the woman, helped her out of her seat, and applied the Heimlich maneuver. A large piece of meat came flying out of the woman's mouth and the woman immediately recovered from the trauma. Hilary came back to the table and calmly finished her meal. The woman she saved was so grateful that she picked up our check and thanked Hilary profusely.

Hilary was pleased with her heroic act, but commented with amusement on the way out of the restaurant, "If I tell my mother that I saved someone's life today, she'll probably ask me why I didn't save two lives."

This critical pattern looks like our rational, healthy ability to critique situations while working toward a higher achievement or goal. It looks similar, but it is very different. Critiquing a situation toward a higher goal will usually result in pleasant feelings, whereas the critical pattern causes a negative vibe, usurping energy and invalidating all who get caught up in it. How many of us have been crushed by hearing over and over again that we were "not good enough," "too intense," etc.? So many have heard their own unique variations while growing up. A large majority of those criticisms have caused so much unnecessary pain and confusion. We no longer have to accept this; there is a way out.

We're all born with an incredible intelligence, a wonderful enthusiasm for life, and an intuitive sense of our complete goodness. We also come into the world with the ability to receive love as well as to give it. We are not born with a critical pattern. In order to survive, however (at least that's what we believed at the time), we unconsciously began to take on some of the patterns of the adults who were close to us. Out of innocence and a pure love for those who were helping us to exist, we began to imitate them, absorbing everything about them that we could, including, unfortunately, their damaged thought processes and their irrational patterns of behavior. It is not necessarily disrespectful to acknowledge that those who cared so deeply for us also passed on to us some distressed perceptions of the world, along with some irrational patterns of behavior. To admit this does not mean that we can't still love them completely.

There are many different types of irrational patterns of behavior, but the common denominator in all of them is this criticalness. Did you ever look at a happy baby when it is looking back at you? Well, that's unconditional love, or a human being without a critical pattern. I believe we were all just like that when we were born, which means that at some point we must have acquired the critical pattern. Assuming that this is true, then, logically, with some new information and a little effort, we should be able to free ourselves from its grip.

A little history. The concept of perfection feeds the critical pattern. We all were conditioned in school to seek perfection, although I believe the schools and teachers were really trying to help students develop a desire for reaching excellence at their own level of potential. All the insecurities and anxieties acquired from years of taking tests strengthened the hold the critical pattern had over us. We were always in fear of failing a test or doing poorly on it. We were often even more terrified of the ridicule and humiliation that came from our peers. The stigma of "a slow child," "stupid," or "dumb" label attached to any student was devastating.

The schools also taught us how to solve problems. This training was essential for our development, but it commonly resulted in students obsessively and compulsively searching for problems to solve. If something was broken, we were encouraged to find what the problem was and to fix it. Some of the better students developed a sharp eye for all the things that weren't "right" in the world. They also developed a sharp criticism of everything that they thought wasn't "the way it should be." As with the sorcerer's apprentice, this ability to find imperfections in others and the world began to get out of control. People with this pattern can't see anything without being critical. This out-of-control critical pattern is just as devastating to the body that it lives in. It criticizes everything the person does and invalidates everything about who they are. The more severe the pattern, the more miserable the person has to be.

Even in the counseling world, there is often more focus on what "the problem is" and "what to do about the problem" than there is on noticing how well we are all doing. I have observed that the more we focus on what's wrong with people, the more we find wrong with them. I have also observed that if we notice what is great about being alive, what's great about being who we are, and what we like about each other, we tend to see more and more of the positive.

If we have a difficult time noticing what is good in our lives, then we are probably being ruled by our critical pattern. It's true that many of us have experienced incredible oppression and horrible physical and emotional abuse, but it's human nature to be able to appreciate what is good about being alive.

Dismantling the Critical Pattern

First of all, we need to understand the way patterns work. An irrational behavior pattern is like an appliance or a light fixture. It doesn't work unless someone turns on the power. Once turned on, it only can do what it is capable of doing. If you turn the light switch on, the light will go on. That's all it can do. When you turn the light switch off, the light goes off. The same is true about a pattern. A negative pattern of behavior could lie dormant for years and have no influence over a person's life, if the person found the way to interrupt the power source that was feeding the pattern. Turn off the light switch and the light turns off and stays off... until someone turns it back on at a later time.

So, the first important step is to find the source of the power: the on/off switch. The best way I've found to find this is to work backwards.

- We need to admit that we have a critical pattern. If we can't admit this, or at least admit that the possibility exists that we have a critical pattern, then no meaningful work can take place.

- We need to understand that the pattern is a separate entity, like a leech, that has camouflaged itself, cleverly integrating itself into our personality. The pattern and the person are different.
- We need to notice what happens to our facial expressions and our body posture when we are in the critical pattern.
- We need to notice the phrases we use that give life to the pattern, along with the tone that we use when we speak the phrases. Make a list of the top ten phrases that you use when you are in the critical pattern. You could have two lists: one for external criticisms and one for internal criticisms. They may or may not be the same.

Example of internal list -

1. "I can't believe you're doing that again."
2. "You're making a fool out of yourself in front of everybody."
3. "Are you sure that's the right decision?"
4. "Why would anybody want to be your friend?"
5. "Look at yourself. You look so stupid in these clothes."

From this point on, whenever you are aware of the critical pattern in action, instead of the phrases, say the number to yourself that corresponds to the phrase on the list. This has a tendency to deflate the power of the phrase. At this point you might start enjoying the dismantling process. It becomes more fun as you go along.

Tell all your friends about your critical pattern and discuss your top ten list with them. This erodes more of the pattern because the habit wants to lurk in the darkness and hide. Talking about it openly and freely contradicts the shame and embarrassment we're made to feel about having the pattern in the first place. Encourage your friends to make their own lists and take some time to act out the pattern, including the facial expressions, the body posture, and the phrases and tone. Be light and have fun with it.

Throughout this process, as you expose the critical pattern as more and more separate from you, the person, you may have strong feelings surface. Allow the body to do its "healing thing" by releasing the emotional toxins stored up over the years, through crying, trembling, raging, and laughter. You'll even find, as the body relieves itself of tension, that big yawns will come out. This is the body relaxing as the tension from the critical pattern drips away.

Memories of loved ones who were critical will probably pop up. These people either criticized you directly or they were seen by you as being very critical. Scan the memories, remembering how you felt back then and what you thought about them. Were they happy or unhappy people?

Notice others with critical patterns. Do they seem like happy people?

Reclaim your power by realizing that you have the free choice, at every moment, to either allow the pattern to run your life or for you to decide to turn its power switch off. Then make the decision to turn it off. In the beginning you may need to repeat this decision a hundred or more times in a day. That's all right. Persevere, and the decision will eventually become permanent.

Throughout the process, appreciate yourself constantly. Cuddle yourself, stroke yourself softly, massage yourself with care. The critical pattern hates it when you're sweet to yourself. It's one of the healthiest and most powerful things you can do to eliminate the negative, critical pattern.

When things are especially difficult, when the critical recordings are running out of control, it's important to combine a few healing tools to reclaim control over your thinking and your life. Three excellent techniques to use here are (1) shifting your point of view, (2) using the power of decision to interrupt the negativity, and (3) setting up a special time everyday to release emotional toxins. Let me explain.

I had a client, Paula, who was going through an incredibly difficult divorce. Her husband of twenty years was doing everything he could to punish her for deciding to leave him. Of course, her husband took no responsibility for his rigid, controlling behavior over the years that might have forced Paula to make her decision.

Paula was valiantly attempting to free herself from a marriage that had gotten too toxic for her to endure. The divorce proceedings were dragging on, with Paula feeling constantly exhausted and overwhelmed. Her internal thoughts were filled with anger, resentment, frustration, helplessness, and confusion. Her health was suffering. She wasn't sleeping well at all and her body was riddled with aches and pains from constant tension.

I pointed out to her that the habitual negativity was depleting her immune system and that she needed to shift her point of view to something more positive. This shift would help her relax a little and boost her immune system.

"I try so hard to think good thoughts," she cried, "but the stuff I'm dealing with is so overwhelming. I try to keep it together but I seem to fall apart everyday around five o'clock" she said. "I just don't know how to do it any other way."

I validated her feelings about the monumental battle she was in. There was no question about it. This woman was being consistently attacked, not physically, but verbally, emotionally, and legally by her abusive husband.

"Paula," I said. "Your situation is horribly abusive. But you still have power in how you let it affect you. I want you to shift your point of view. As bad as things are, there are lots of things that you can be grateful for. I'd like you to notice how lucky you are to be alive. Every morning when you wake up, say to yourself, "Paula, you are a very lucky woman." Use your attention to notice the places where you are truly lucky. In spite of all the suffering you are going through, there are still lots of ways you are really fortunate."

She thought for awhile and got very quiet, then said, "You know, you're right. I am very smart, I'm pretty healthy, and I am not starving."

I then said, "And you're living in a very safe neighborhood, you've got two very healthy children, and you love to go on long walks in the woods."

She smiled, relaxed a little, and found a few more things that proved to her that she was truly a lucky woman.

"So, you're saying if I begin the day with this positive statement about how lucky I am, and then notice places where it's actually true, that will help shift my attention away from always obsessing about all the crap that's going on."

"That's right," I said. "You have the ability to shift your attention to focus on things that will strengthen your immune system, rather than focusing on stuff that keeps draining you and exhausting your body."

I pointed out to her that this would not be a simple task, based on all the years of conditioning which trained her to focus on negative thoughts. I also pointed out that she was completely capable of achieving this shift.

The second aspect would be that she needed to interrupt the critical recordings whenever she was aware that they were running in her head.

"When you notice the critical recordings are running, you need to stop them immediately and decide again to shift your attention away from the negative and toward the positive—in this case, the statement that you are a very lucky woman."

I told her that to be successful she may need to interrupt the negative recordings a lot in the beginning, maybe as much as fifty to a hundred times in a day, and keep making the decision to shift her attention to how lucky she was.

"I'll do my best," she said quietly, while seemingly deep in thought, "but, to be completely honest with you, it feels like it might be a little pretentious."

"Pretense," I explained, "is a state that arises from constantly denying that there is anything wrong. That's not what you'll be doing here. You're well aware of the difficulties going on in your life. You're not attempting to deny that or hide from it in any way. What you are doing is just acknowledging the difficulties that exist, but then choosing to not obsess about them. Or, in other words, you're making an aware decision to shift your focus of attention away from the difficulties and toward something that is more useful. It's not helpful to obsess about the garbage. If it were, I'd encourage you to focus on it. But the truth is, it doesn't help a bit and, in fact, it causes more toxins to build up in the body."

"I think I understand about the critical recordings, but what about all the feelings?" she inquired. "It seems like I'm always building up all this emotional tension on a daily basis from this divorce. I keep trying to suppress it so I can function during the day, but it's so much work trying to keep it together."

"If you discipline yourself to start each day with the focus on the fact that you are a lucky woman and make the decision to interrupt the negative recordings anytime you are aware of them," I explained further, "then you will begin to have a smaller and smaller build-up of emotional tension each day. The feeling like you're going to explode with emotions will slowly diminish. But, it's true, you will still need a special time for allowing your body to release any stored-up emotional tensions."

Since Paula had earlier mentioned the five o'clock hour as a time where she usually "lost it," I encouraged her to set aside that hour everyday as her special time to give her body the chance to release. I encouraged her to find a friend who could listen to her with respect and compassion for that hour on a few of the days. I invited her to be accepting of the tears, the raging, the terror, and whatever else she might need to feel and release during the hour. I then recommended that she look forward to that hour for release purposes. That was to be her special time. I explained to her that this space could not be compromised if she wanted good results.

Paula was in the middle of a horrible divorce that was clearly toxic to her life. However, with these tools she had a chance to use her intelligence to minimize negative effects.

CHAPTER 2: Greed

Leaving the womb and coming into this world brings up many problems for the newborn child. He or she is thrust from an existence where every need is taken care of into an unknown world with lots of uncertainty. Breathing is the first major hurdle, but then other needs arise quickly—needs like warmth, closeness, nourishment, and sleep. A baby's survival is in jeopardy if any of these needs aren't met.

Most of us, as completely dependent and vulnerable babies, experienced lots of times when our needs were not met immediately. This had to be terrifying to us.

A baby is either safe, secure and tranquil, or in need of something. If its needs are not met immediately, a baby experiences the physical body with increasing discomfort and depletion. Some of the effects from this deprivation are devastating and long-lasting.

As an example, lots of people born between 1946 and 1964, the "baby-boomer" generation, were fed every four hours, according to the best medical thinking of that time. Millions of those babies probably needed nourishment before the four hours were up, and some probably didn't need the nourishment quite that soon. Physical deprivation was experienced by those who needed food more quickly than four hours. The baby's survival was at stake, with the child never knowing if nourishment would ever come again.

Some of those babies who are grown adults today still have major food struggles. But more important for most of us is what happens when we feel deprivation in the present. Any time we experience emotional deprivation, a trigger goes off in the body reminding us of the earliest memory of deprivation. This is why some people act like they are going to die if they don't immediately get whatever it is that they want. It looks quite dramatic but, in effect, they are truly re-experiencing the pain, fear, desperation, and confusion that they felt a long time ago as babies.

We do all sorts of things to avoid feeling deprived. In fact, a large portion of our irrational, greedy behavior is directly connected to early feelings of want. The unconscious pull is to keep acquiring more possessions, money, lovers, etc., as a buffer, a protection from those old, painful feelings of deprivation.

I knew a very successful electrician named Jack, who owned his own company. He had a closet full of expensive, new, unwrapped underwear. At first I thought this was very strange and, on some level, I questioned his sanity. Then I found out about his background.

Jack had been very poor as a child. His family was so poor that his parents very often didn't have enough money to buy him underwear. This was terribly humiliating to young Jack and he swore to have enough money one day to have a hundred sets of underwear.

I've counseled many people who did not want to look at the

early feelings of deprivation they experienced as children. Initially they did not understand the connection between those old feelings and their irrational drives and insatiable desires in the present. It was easier for them to keep chasing carrots and struggling with problems in the moment, even though they all admitted that their achievements and successes did not give them much real satisfaction. No matter how much they acquired, it never felt like enough.

No matter how much some people eat, it will never feel like enough. For some people it will never feel like there's time to rest. The urgency, the desperation, the irrational drives will persist, unless we make the decision to face uncomfortable emotions. If we face the feelings of deprivation and release the emotional toxins, we can then free ourselves from the obsessive and compulsive behaviors that rule our lives.

I met Johnny, a thirty-five-year-old man, at a workshop some years ago. He and his girlfriend Fran were struggling with some issues and they wanted some help from me. I listened to both of them as they cried and raged about their frustrations and pain.

Fran felt manipulated by Johnny. "Whatever Johnny wants, Johnny must have," she said. She said that no matter what it was, her boyfriend acted like he would die if he didn't get it. Fran said his behavior gave her no room to breathe in the relationship, and, although she loved Johnny, she couldn't continue to go on like this anymore.

His point of view was a little different. "Every time I ask for something she makes it out to be a big deal. She hems and haws and I start feeling really bad, like I'm gonna die if I don't get it. I don't know why, but I feel like my survival's at stake and she's got all the controls."

After working with them for awhile, it became clear that

Johnny had some deep distress from early childhood deprivation that was running his life. When we began, he thought Fran was controlling him and he was angry at her. By the time we ended the session, he understood that his life was being controlled, but not by Fran. It was being run by his old feelings of deprivation. We explored this in detail in the session and discovered a few interesting insights. Johnny's parents were poor when he was young, and both of them had to work. He remembered lots of times when he was starving, cold, and alone, waiting for them to come home. He also mentioned that his parents were Holocaust survivors, possibly a reason that he literally felt like his survival was at stake when the feelings of deprivation arose.

Johnny cried in the session, remembering the early pain and just how hard it really used to be for him. He stopped blaming Fran and took some responsibility by promising to talk to her about his difficult past whenever he felt deprived.

When Fran heard this, she also started crying. She talked about how much she really loved Johnny, and how much she wanted their relationship to work. She also talked about how bad it felt to be seen as a "controlling bitch." She knew it wasn't true, but she was beginning to doubt herself. Fran cried when talking about all the years of being leered at by men and how bad that made her feel about herself. She mentioned a few memories where men were relentlessly pushing themselves on her, demanding sex and always wanting more from her.

After raging for a good chunk of time about the injustices she suffered as a woman, she became quieter and more thoughtful. Fran then took Johnny's hand and said that she would work toward being more compassionate in regard to Johnny's struggles and, hopefully, become less apt to slip into reacting rigidly to some of his demands.

When Johnny and Fran ended the counseling session with me, they had reclaimed their ability to see the goodness and innocence in each other. They were able to see where their unhealed areas of emotional tension were entangling. They had new information about how to maintain flexible thinking when the old pain might surface, and they had a renewed sense of hope. Their patterns of behavior were clearly exposed as old parasites, rigidly hanging on. They could see the difference between the present and the past; the difference between the reality of the situation and the way their painful feelings distorted their perception of that reality. They still had lots of work to do, but were finally unstuck, and excited about their new awareness.

Releasing emotional toxins stored up over the years from painful experiences of deprivation will undoubtedly shift your outlook on life. Compulsive behavior based on the feelings of greed will gradually diminish. Your body will become more relaxed. You'll notice that your attention span will increase and your ability to focus and complete goals will undoubtedly improve.

- Make the decision to look at the places in your life where you feel deprived.
- Then, with awareness and intention, allow yourself to feel the painful emotions when one of these situations arises in the present. Remember, the immediate reaction will be to speed up and run away from the place of painful emotions. This is your sign to do the opposite. Slow down, take a few breaths and look at the situation that is triggering your reaction. Some people, because of the unique way they were hurt in the past, will react in a different way. They will, instead of speeding up, freeze in their bodies, becoming

quiet and stiff. They will have a tendency to "leave their bodies," in effect, and come back when it's safer. Both are reactions of fear. They each are a form of leaving: one leaves physically, the other leaves in the only way they know how, spiritually. The one who speeds up is reacting in a "scared active" way, while the other is reacting in a "scared passive" way. For those who react in scared passive ways, first make the decision to stay in your body and not leave. Then make sure you keep moving your body. This will help you stay grounded and connected to your physicalness.

- If you feel you have safety and the support of others, allow yourself to release some of the emotional toxins that will bubble up. If you don't have this safety in the moment, take a visual picture in your mind's eye of the whole scene, then recall the scene when you feel safer and have the attention of a close friend who will listen to you in a non-judgmental way.

- Scan your memory for earlier times in your past when you remember feeling the same way.

- Think of what you needed in the past that would have been fulfilling and satisfying.

- Acknowledge to yourself that if you had received the support you needed back then, you would not be struggling with the same intensity of feeling in the present.

- Decide to inhibit any irrational behavior that might be set into motion by old feelings of deprivation. This is crucial. If you can interrupt any pulls to go ballistic, you in effect lay the groundwork for real healing. It's okay if you need to remind yourself—a hundred times a day, if necessary—of this powerful decision.

- Appreciate yourself for becoming more in charge of your

life, and for being able to see the difference between you, the wonderful person, and your distresses. This is an essential step in the healing process and the tendency will be to minimize the work you've done. Remember to appreciate yourself well!

CHAPTER 3: Jealousy

ↄ∾ↄ

Isabel was seething. She had just come back from a simple walk to the store, but there was no escape. It seemed like everywhere she went they would appear—happy mothers with their new-born babies. Isabel had turned forty last month and desperately wanted her own child. She strongly believed that her life would have no real meaning unless she brought a baby into the world. Her mother was no help either. She was getting older and kept asking Isabel when she was going to give her a grandchild.

Isabel could hear her biological clock ticking, her mother's not-so-dignified inquiries, and her own internal dialogue. It was all driving her crazy. She hated herself for the abortion she had twelve years before. She didn't think much about it back then, but now she wasn't so sure it didn't have something to do with her two miscarriages in the last three years. She wasn't sure about a lot of things anymore. But one thing she knew; she always was feeling jealous rage toward new mothers. She felt cursed. She was furious with God and she hated herself and her life more and more everyday.

How many times have you heard of people flipping into a jealous rage, hurting themselves or others? How many times have you felt out of control with jealous feelings? Did you do something that you regretted? Did you have to keep yourself from getting into an argument or from getting out on the road and driving dangerously? Did you ever hurt yourself or another person because of a jealous rage? Have you ever done drugs or alcohol to numb yourself so you wouldn't have to feel those pangs of jealousy?

The definition of jealousy is "to feel resentment or envy toward someone's successes, achievements, or advantages." The definition is accurate as far as observing and identifying the state of mind of someone who is feeling this emotion. However, in no way does this definition assist you in your search to understand the cause and learn how to cleanse yourself from its irrational effects.

On the surface, jealousy is fueled by external experiences. We see things or people that we feel jealous toward and we burn with envy or resentment inside. The big mistake for those who feel jealous is to keep focusing on the external. When you are feeling jealous, you are usually feeling bad about yourself. You are usually feeling a combination of fear, self-criticism, and some form of deprivation.

We tend to be jealous of someone who has more money and can buy fancier cars, clothes, or the latest hot item on the market. We tend to be jealous of people who we think are more physically attractive, more financially successful, more successful in their work, more recognized and well-respected, or whatever. This is clearly the result of you feeling that you are "less than" in all those areas. If you feel that you are not enough, then you will be compelled to feel jealous of those you think have more.

There will always be people who have more than you. So, the real problem is not about attempting to acquire more things, money, lovers, etc. No, the problem is internal, and nothing external that you do or achieve will ever permanently free you from feeling the painful emotion that you are trying to avoid.

Even if Isabel had the baby she so desperately wanted, she'd sooner or later find something wrong in her life that would trigger those jealous feelings again. Maybe, in her mind, other babies would appear easier to care for or other new moms would appear to have so much more help from their friends than she was receiving. Her jealous feelings would find a way to keep making her feel miserable about her life.

Years ago, I counseled two very different people on their feelings of jealousy. Pete was a successful businessman from Wall Street, while Mike was an unemployed musician. Although Pete had a few million dollars to his name, he still felt jealous of the "big boys in the game," as he put it. He complained about not having the kind of money needed to really be a powerful influence.

Mike, on the other hand, was jealous of a couple of his friends in the music world who had made it big. He was constantly putting himself down for not being as successful as they were.

Both of these men felt scared, insecure, critical of themselves, and deprived. I worked with both of them on feeling the feelings and releasing the emotional toxins they had stored up. They released in different ways, but the results were similar. Jealousy slowly became a non-issue. They learned to notice the pure feelings of fear, sadness, and deprivation under the complex emotion of jealousy. They both learned to slow down, to release the emotional toxins when it was safe to do so, to be around friends who cared more about them than what they accomplished, and to notice the qualities they liked about themselves.

In general, if you are feeling jealous:

- Stop fantasizing about what others have that you don't have. You may need to make this decision over and over again before you conquer the pattern's pull to focus on the external. If you continue to concentrate on others and what they have that you don't have, you feed the irrational flames of jealousy.

- Interrupt all forms of self-criticism. There is nothing useful about criticizing yourself when you are in this state of mind. It only makes you feel worse about yourself and undermines what confidence you still have. (Refer to the chapter on understanding and cleansing your mind of self-criticism.)

- Allow yourself to slow down enough to feel the feelings of deprivation. You can do this alone, but the process works better when you can be with someone who cares about you. Remember to inform them about what you need from them, whether it's a warm hug or a good listening ear. Do your best to refuse the pull to ask for advice when you're in the struggle, and firmly reject any offers of advice as well. It really isn't what you need. If they are good friends, they will respect your requests and come through for you.

- Release the emotional toxins that will surface. Remember, your body will know what to do. Your job is to give it the space it needs to heal. Observe your body while it is in the process of releasing emotional toxins. Notice the relief your body experiences as the releasing is taking place. After you release, you will usually feel calmer and more grounded, especially if you interrupt any negative recordings that might be judging, condemning, or invalidating the body's healing process.

- Appreciate yourself for having the courage to look within, rather than compulsively and obsessively continuing to chase external carrots.

A large part of our lives is spent relating to other people. Jealous feelings are bound to arise at some point in your relationships. It's useful to see the surfacing of jealous feelings as an opportunity to do some emotional cleansing, releasing old stored up emotional toxins from the past, while deepening your connection with another human being. The key piece here is that both people are willing to listen to each other and work together.

Years ago my partner and I were struggling with a problem. She wanted to work closely with Jamie, a good-natured, sensitive man, on a project that was going to be exciting to her. I wanted her to enjoy this opportunity, but I was terrified about her working so closely with Jamie. For one reason or another I felt jealous, insecure, and deeply threatened by their friendship. I couldn't think of anything but their growing connection, and it was disrupting my days, interfering with my sleep and my health.

We needed to go to a therapist for some help because we both felt extremely upset and backed into corners. She did not want to give up her exciting opportunity, and I, no matter how hard I tried, couldn't come to terms with my jealous feelings about her and this other guy.

The therapy was useful. After both of us had a chance to yell and scream at each other with supervision, we were thoughtfully guided toward sharing the more vulnerable content that was underneath all the anger.

We found a place where we could listen to each other with respect, share our raw feelings, and respond thoughtfully from a deeply caring place, rather than from a self-centered place of disappointment and deprivation. I heard how important this job was to her. She heard how all my insecurities were surfacing because of her growing friendship with Jamie. We acknowledged that we still did love each other and that we both wanted to come up with a healthy plan that would work for both of us.

We did. I promised to work hard on the jealousy and insecurity so that I could get to a place where I could be completely supportive to the project and her friendship with Jamie. She promised to pull back from the project for six weeks, which helped me restore my confidence in our loving connection.

It was just what I needed, and in only three weeks I felt confident enough to cheer her on completely. She was relieved, thrilled, and delighted to have our loving connection restored, and just as excited as ever about starting the project. She worked on the project with Jamie for a few years, with no other difficulties surfacing between us.

CHAPTER 4: Depression
~~~

I counseled a woman over several years who was struggling with chronic depression. At first, she talked about being depressed because she always felt disappointed in herself and her life. She also felt hopeless about ever living life without feeling this deep disappointment. She had achieved lots of goals—a good husband, a beautiful baby, a cozy home, and a good job. But the disappointment leaked out everywhere and made it impossible for her to notice that her life was good.

Instead of taking prescription drugs, probably some mood-elevators, she decided to work on the problem from an emotional point of view. I first helped her distinguish between her depression and the feelings of disappointment and hopelessness. Of course she was depressed. Anybody would be depressed if they felt hopeless about ever getting out of a lousy situation. But depression, from my point of view, is just a state of mind that we get into when we can't figure out what to do to make things better.

More and more people are experiencing overwhelming challenges in their lives and identifying the resulting state of mind as depression. The fast, high-powered pace of our society is constant-ly pushing us toward greater and greater expectations, desires that are often unreasonable and rarely attainable for individuals. Some people find themselves mired in what appears to be endless emo-tional turmoil. They feel like they are treading water in a sea of emotions with no end in sight. This picture is exhausting and can be quite depressing. Others have been trained to be cut off from their emotional bodies, without any means of releasing the build-up of emotional toxins. Their everyday lives are difficult, with the per-ception that there is very little hope for a better life in the future. Both scenarios can be seen as depressing.

The medical profession, along with the drug companies, encour-age people who are depressed to begin treatment with drugs. My observation is that drugs given for emotional imbalances, on occa-sion, and only if taken on a temporary basis, can sometimes benefit the person. Most of the time, however, drugs numb out the person, disconnecting them even further from their emotional body, and adding another layer of distress. People on mood-altering drugs may appear to be more docile and may actually be easier for others to spend time with on a short-term basis, but the drugs are masking the real problem, not making it better.

I, obviously, direct people away from the world of drugs and numbness. I encourage people to reclaim their ability to feel all their emotions, especially the painful ones, learn how to release the stored up emotional toxins, and reconnect to their power. It's easi-er to take a pill and "forget about it," and everybody certainly has the freedom to choose what path they walk down. But those peo-ple who choose the path away from drugs and toward human con-nection keep open the possibility of a vibrant, wholesome future. I do not think it is possible to achieve this kind of meaningful life while on drugs.

I encouraged my client to talk about the disappointment that she felt. She talked quietly and shyly at first, a little embarrassed about revealing her struggle. When she noticed I was relaxed and interested, she became more animated and began to go a little deeper. Tears, shaking, and raging ensued, interspersed with periods of talking with more enthusiasm. We were beginning to unravel the ball of distress.

We worked for a few weeks on releasing the emotional toxins attached to the deep disappointment, instead of trying to figure out a solution to the problem. She scanned earlier memories in her past when she felt disappointed. Then one day, through some tears, she stopped and turned to me. She said, "You know, my father wanted so badly to be a millionaire but he never made it. For years he walked around disappointed with his life." She was quiet and calm, with lots of thoughts rushing around her brain. Then she remembered a few times at a very young age when she had been happy and not disappointed at all. Again she spoke. "I loved my father so much. I used to play with him sometimes to try to get him out of feeling so bad. Most of the time I failed. But I wasn't disappointed then. He was and I wasn't."

It didn't take her long to realize that, at that early age, she took on her father's disappointment. It was his, not hers. With this new piece of information, she was able to intellectually and emotionally separate from the negative effects of this "attitude of disappointment." She was well on her way to healing. She still had work to do, but she had a renewed enthusiasm for her life. The depression was completely gone. The feeling of hopelessness disappeared early in the counseling work. She now had two clear jobs—to keep doing the emotional work, and to remember that most of the time, if she felt deeply disappointed, it was probably her father's old disappointment, not hers.

All too often in our society we try to fix what appears to be the immediate problem at hand. It's a reasonable attitude, but often it does not work. This is because the real problem is that the person needs to release emotional toxins, stored up from past hurtful experiences.

Deep disappointment along with hopelessness are often the underlying distresses beneath the surface of a depressed person. However, it doesn't matter what the feelings are underneath the layer of depression. The key is that the person is numbed out or shut down because they have been unable to get in touch with their emotional body, and as a result have been unable to release emotional toxins.

Those who are mired in a sea of emotions, on the other hand, are feeling intensely, but something is preventing the emotional toxins from being released. Once again, it's important here to clarify that feelings are not emotional toxins.

"No expectations, no disappointments?" I have seen many people give up their life-long dreams and goals in an attempt to circumvent feeling disappointment. Maybe it's not a bad idea for some people whose lives seem to be in constant turmoil because of their unmanageable emotions. This book, however, is offering what I believe to be a much healthier approach.

The problem is not about avoiding the painful feeling of disappointment or, for that matter, any other painful emotion. The real problem appears to be people's inability to understand their own emotions, and to handle those emotions in a way that will release toxins and actually enhance their lives.

I encourage you to rationally assess your dreams and then, if they seem reasonable, to cherish them. I encourage you to set goals for your life. I encourage you to allow yourself to be excited again, just as you used to be when you were a child. I also encourage you to understand that most of us will not reach all of our goals. Some of us will not have many of our dreams come true. If some of your goals and dreams have not been met, I encourage you to feel the disappointment, to cry about the busted bubble, to rage about the inequities in life. I encourage you to feel fully the painful emotions, then to release the buildup of emotional toxins and, finally, to come out on the other side. This is what emotional growth is all about.

If you think you are depressed and wish to shift this attitude:

- Take a few minutes to write down the things about your life that are bringing you down. Some of us have difficult lives while others have relatively easy lives. In most situations depression exists because of how someone feels about their life regardless of its actual ease or difficulty. It doesn't do much good to make judgements about whose life is more difficult. However, it is useful to get clear about the specific things that are causing you to feel so lousy.
- If there are places in your life where you are being abused, invalidated, or disrespected, you need to figure out how to get yourself out of this negative situation, one way or another, without hurting yourself or anybody else. This is possible, although it may feel hopeless. The feeling of hopelessness almost always exists in people who experience depression.
- For many, depression is like a layer of numbness that locks in all the emotional toxins that need to be released. It's like an old pile of cow manure that has formed a crusty layer on the surface. If you put a pitchfork to the pile you will find that under the hard crusty surface there is softer, smelly stuff. Get through the hard, dead layer of depression and you will always find that unwieldy pile of emotional toxins,

which, in a sense, is like the manure, usually pretty messy and smelly. But that's also where your life's juice lies, waiting to be reclaimed. Ask yourself, "What emotions might I feel if I stripped away that thick, crusty layer of depression?"

- The feelings, thoughts and emotional toxins that may surface can be quite intense and confusing. Here's where you need to be smart. If you can handle releasing these toxins on your own, then you're on your way toward freeing yourself from your depressed state. If you find that the intensity is too overwhelming, then you need to find a private counselor or therapist to give you guidance through the storm of emotions. Support groups that are focused on releasing emotions are also useful. The key here is that you are honest with yourself. If you can handle this stuff on your own, great. If not, get help.

- Remember, this releasing takes time and you may not immediately see huge shifts in your life. Persist with the cleansing process, however. It will pay off for you in the long run. After each time that you release some emotional toxins, come up with some way of being kind to yourself, appreciating your courage for tackling this difficulty. Ask yourself, "How can I be good to myself in ways that are healthy for me?"

CHAPTER 5: Abuse
∽∽∽

If you're not depressed or numbed out, and you're frequently feeling intense emotions as a result of wounds from the present or the past, you may have a tendency toward irrational, aggressive behavior.

Have you ever been betrayed by a good friend or a family member? Have you ever experienced the confusion, pain, outrage and shock that takes place when you realize that you've been betrayed? Well, many of us have experienced abuse which we often don't even consider as a betrayal. Large numbers of children were often spanked as a form of discipline, and, to this day, there are thousands of kids who are currently going through varying degrees of physical abuse by their parents. Sometimes this abuse is rationalized by the parents as their best attempt at disciplining their children. Other times it's just a flagrant, irrational act of violence, intimidation, and domination. In both cases, these parents are oblivious to the fact that they are betraying their children, inflicting physical damage, and destroying the trust in their cherished relationship. Most of the time this violent behavior by parents is an unconscious repetition of the kind of treatment they received when they were young. However, this is no excuse for continuing irrational behavior. A couple of years ago, I spent an interesting evening with some old friends. We were five adults hanging out together, reminiscing about the "good old days" in the early seventies. Two of my friends, Elaine and Dinah, had brought their children along, and the kids were playing in another room. Nine-year-old Penny, Elaine's daughter, and seven-year-old Josh, Dinah's son, were getting along just fine, peacefully playing Monopoly when we all decided to go into town for some food.

I had brought over a huge tin can filled with popcorn for everybody to enjoy, but instead we all decided to save it for an after-dinner snack. The kids wanted to stay home and continue their game, and both mothers thought it would be all right. However, both Elaine and Dinah insisted firmly to their children that the popcorn not be opened while we were gone. The kids reluctantly agreed.

About an hour later we five adults strolled into the house with hot Chinese food from one of the restaurants in town. Penny and Josh both greeted us in a funny, slightly embarrassed way, and immediately all the adults knew something was up. Elaine walked into the kid's room and noticed a few popcorn kernels on the rug. Then she lifted up the rug and found big piles of popcorn—hundreds of little kernels everywhere. I thought it was kind of funny and began to laugh. Elaine was pissed off though, and demanded an explanation from Penny and Josh. My laughter turned to quiet astonishment as I observed the different behavior of the two children. Both Penny and Josh knew they had been caught red-handed and would have to "fess up" and deal with the consequences. Penny, taking a defensive but somewhat apologetic attitude, went into an elaborate explanation about just how the popcorn ended up under the rug. Josh, on the other hand, was quiet as a mouse, trembling in the corner, as if anticipating some horrible punishment.

Dinah had a history of punishing her son with spankings and occasionally hit him out of the blue when she was having a hard day. Elaine, on the other hand, never hit her daughter. The results were as obvious as night and day.

If you are physically abusive to your children, or for that matter, to anyone you are close to, you are causing major damage to that person you supposedly "love," as well as to your relationship with that person. There is no longer any doubt about the effects of this kind of abuse.

Physical abuse is all about control, domination, and intimidation. It has no place in any relationship that is based on respect and caring.

If you have a pattern of being physically abusive, you probably have a mind-set that rationalizes the need for being that way. You probably also have an attitude that minimizes the negative effect of the abuse. This is not your fault, although at this point in your life it is your responsibility to stop your irrational behavior and clean up this destructive part of your life. It's also probably true that you were abused as a child and actually believed, on some level, that your parents had good reason to hit you. Well, you never deserved to be hit. I'll say it again. You never deserved to be hit, no matter what weird stuff you might have done. Those who hit you were wrong. Physical abuse can often lead to terrible damage to a person in a number of ways. It never does any good!

When the human body experiences physical abuse, on a mental level there is incredible confusion; on an emotional level there is outrage, hurt, and fear; and on a physical level there is muscle constriction and an immediate triggering of the sympathetic nervous system—the fight/flight response. The body knows that this is not only wrong, but sees physical abuse as a direct threat to its survival. There is nothing about any kind of physical abuse that supports any part of health and well-being.

If you experienced physical abuse as a child you will have, inside of your being, a pull to either be abusive or to be abused. When the abuse happened in the past, emotions were high. Therefore, on occasion in the present, when emotions become intense, the abusive pattern of behavior could very well appear.

Here are a few helpful ways to insure that you don't get caught up in repeating the abusive pattern of behavior.

- You can count to ten very slowly or take a few deep breaths. This will help you interrupt the "scared active" pull of the pattern to act out a very toxic, destructive scene.
- You can immediately stop the dialogue between you and the person you're engaged with, that might be causing the anger to boil up. If you decide to leave the scene, tell your friend when you will be back. This is important information for the other person to have, and will help to maintain the respect between both of you. This responsible behavior will be an important aid in defusing the scene.
- You can call another friend and spend some time on the phone. Inform your phone buddy about what is going on. The pull will be to hide the fact that you feel like being physically abusive. Most people feel incredible shame for this sort of behavior. This reaction of shame is more indication that, on some level, we all know it is wrong. Taking the initiative to tell another person will, most of the time, insure that abuse does not happen. If the other person has any skills in listening, he or she will help you find a way to cool down.

- You could hit a bed or a pillow as much as you want. This often helps get some of the intense energy out. Yelling at the bed or the walls might help move the energy as well. Getting the tension released is crucial, and although the pull will be to direct the yelling and hitting toward the person whom you care about, the bed and the walls will serve you better. You won't end up feeling that guilty if you yell at the walls and hit the bed.
- You could get behind a drum set and beat the hell out of the drums without destroying anything. This can be satisfying and will also tend to shift the energy.

There are probably about five hundred ways to move the energy without being destructive. The previous five are just some simple examples. If they are not right for you, find others that will work for you. The key is that you don't allow the destructive pattern to run you. You do have the power to interrupt your irrational behavior. There is no question about this. You just need to make the decision to stop. You'll probably need some help, especially in the beginning. But if you really want to stop the irrational behavior, you can and will take responsibility to set up support for yourself.

Another key is that you need to get the energy out. Inhibiting and suppressing the energy will just leave you all wound up. Sooner or later you will need to release it. Remember, you are not bad and the energy is not bad. Getting it out in a constructive way is part of the healing process at work.

At some point it would probably make sense to get some professional assistance with these kinds of toxic patterns of behavior. They are filled with emotional toxins that need to be released, and inevitably will be released if the violent behavior is curtailed. It's possible to do this work on your own, but releasing these toxins effectively is more likely if you have a skilled professional working with you.

Making the decision to get help for your own health and well-being is so much more satisfying than being shamed or guilted into seeking help by friends or relatives—or being ordered to by the courts. Similarly, in the world of medicine, people who choose to have elective surgery are statistically more successful than those who must have emergency surgery. You can go to a therapist or join a support group for a limited period of time to dismantle this pattern. This can be an admirable decision and a true act of love for yourself. It's a statement that you want a better life and that you are willing to do some work to make a positive change. In many cases, it's making the decision to interrupt an abusive pattern of behavior that has been passed on for generations. If you successfully stop the passing on of abuse, it is no small accomplishment. You are actually changing history and have every right to take complete pride in yourself.

Another form of physical abuse, although much more subtle, is the constant pull to disregard what you are physically feeling. The human body is an incredibly finely tuned, intelligent, amazingly resilient form of life. If we stay in touch with our body, it will, time and time again, lead us to health and well-being. The human body is magically constructed to heal itself. But we, in this arrogant culture, continually disregard or distort the simple information that we receive from our bodies. Many of us have gotten so disconnected from our physical selves that we don't even know what our bodies are feeling or how to interpret the information. This is sad.

I had a friend who came down with breast cancer a few years ago. Her first reaction was anger. She felt totally betrayed by her body. The truth was that she had been betraying her body every day for most of her life. Her conditioning confused her into ignoring her body's attempts to heal through emotional release. She suppressed all that because she had been embarrassed into feeling bad about her body functions. Over the years she had done drugs, caffeine, nicotine, some alcohol, and used lots of cosmetics, all in an attempt to be accepted by the crowd she hung out with. After years and years of valiant attempts to heal itself from the constant barrage of toxic assaults, her body began to break down.

The cancer was a wake-up call. This courageous woman went through surgery, did lots of emotional work that helped her alter her values and priorities, changed her diet completely, began a conscious exercise program to strengthen her muscular/skeletal system and became sensitized to her body. She heeded the wake-up call, did the work that she had to do, and is, today, living well and teaching what she learned to other women who have become inflicted with cancer. One of her greatest frustrations, she says, is that there are so many people who can still have a good life in spite of the cancer, but don't take their healing seriously. She's told me that she has seen so many people die—not from the cancer, she believes strongly, but from their stubborn rigidity in refusing to give up the kind of lifestyle and patterns of behavior that may have helped cause the cancer in the first place.

For you to reclaim the kind of sensitivity to your body that I'm talking about here, you first need to make the decision to do it. Making this choice will always help you focus on your goal. If you take your intent seriously, positive results will often follow. Next, you need to refuse any pull by society that encourages you to betray your body. Listen to your body. If something is not right, it will tell you. The more you listen, the more you will develop—or should I say reclaim—your inherent ability to hear. Everything else will, in time, fall into place on your quest for health and a more connected life. One major drawback to this process, however, is that you will probably no longer enjoy socializing with old friends who want to maintain an abusive, disconnected lifestyle. These people will also probably do their unintentional best to derail your best attempts at healing. Although it will be quite sobering, my only advice here is to kiss the old group good-bye and start seeking out people who will cheer you on toward health.

At some point in this process, if you're fortunate, you will reclaim your emotional connection to loving your own body. This can be a profound moment in your life. We all have betrayed our physical beings to varying degrees in our lifetimes. If we can get in touch with this deep love we were born with and still have for our bodies, then we will be primed for powerful healing at some point in the near future, probably when we least expect it. When this time arrives, there may be lots of warm tears, releasing toxins from deep pools of grief stored up for years. From this moment on, you most likely will begin to treat your body with a new respect.

Your body is a precious palace and the home of your spirit. Your body needs to be loved, respected, listened to, trusted, and cared for on a daily basis. You can enjoy having a better spiritual connection when you are connected emotionally and physically. In addition, your ability to consciously love your friends as well as receive love from your friends will be greatly enhanced.

CHAPTER 6: Guilt

∾∾∾

The Jewish mother listened patiently to her son as the young man timidly explained to her that he was going to marry his African-American girlfriend. After doing his best to convince her that he was truly happy for the first time in his life, he paused, nervously waiting for her approval.

"Don't worry about me, my beautiful son," she said looking ashen and deeply disappointed. "If I die in my sleep tonight, well, I don't want you to think it has anything to do with your decision."

A subtle and more sophisticated form of control and manipulation is guilt. However, guilt is nothing less than non-violent abuse. Have you ever had a "guilt trip" laid on you? Do you remember how it felt? Can you remember any of the words, tones, and facial expressions of the person who was trying to make you feel guilty? Was it effective? Did you give in to the demands or did you act defiantly, refusing to give in? Did you know that either response meant that you were hooked?

Or are you someone who lays guilt trips on people? Are you

aware that you do this? Do you remember where you learned this? Do you know that you can change this kind of behavior if you choose? Do you want to?

I believe that we were all born with an innate knowledge of right and wrong, good and bad. We all were born with the understanding that killing or harming others, especially those more vulnerable, is wrong. We all were born with the knowledge of equality and sharing. If we all had been allowed to nurture and develop our emotional bodies, this deep, inherent understanding would still be intact in all of us. We would not be susceptible to subtle manipulation through guilt. However, the vast majority of us as very young children went through a methodical, albeit unaware, stripping of our connection to this inherent understanding by the adults who did their best to care for us. Our healing processes, which insured our connection, were stifled and inhibited, confusing us about our humanity. Then, we were fed a constant barrage of misinformation about the world, once again innocently passed on by those who loved us, and were encouraged to chase the disconnected desires of society.

The obvious and most effective way to reclaim our lost connection and free ourselves from guilt is to work toward reclaiming a strong understanding of our emotional body. I've observed, time and time again, that those who make friends with and understand their emotions become more deeply connected to their humanity. Our emotions are like the roots to our tree, the deeper and more well-nourished they are, the stronger and taller our tree can grow. Those who reclaim their inherent qualities know the difference between right and wrong. Those who don't have this connection are much more apt to be lost and are often doomed to be influenced by and follow anyone or any group of people that "appears to know." This can be dangerous.

Reclaiming our inherent connection gives us an incredible advantage in finding and sustaining a healthy life. As in the following story about Joseph, it gives us a deep, calm sense of knowing, when others may be frantic and scattered in their search to find answers.

Joseph had lunch with God and then went into town. He noticed a large group of people involved in a heated discussion. He quietly approached them and sat down at the back of the gathering, listening to the content of their discussion. They were arguing, each side trying to convince the other that their point of view was the correct one. The issue was, "Does God exist?" None of them knew the answer, but they were all arguing with passion and conviction. Joseph listened for awhile, remembered lunch, smiled softly to himself, then peacefully walked on.

In the counseling world, we find the effects of guilt to be pretty devastating to all those afflicted with the "curse." A guilt trip is simply one person's attempt, conscious or unconscious, to get another person to comply with what they want. It is a subtle form of control and manipulation, designed to confuse and enslave the recipient. Very often, people get hooked by the guilt trip regardless of their response, whether they comply or react defiantly.

Two sisters were raised by their mother, who did her darndest to make them comply with her wishes. When the sisters were young, she constantly lectured to them. "I know what's best for you girls," she'd say sternly. "And remember, every time you don't follow what I want for you, well, you might as well be putting a knife through my heart. I love you both so much and I know you'll always do the right thing, and that's what your mother wants for you."

Amy, the older sister, really believed that her mother would have a heart attack or get cancer if she didn't follow in her mother's footsteps. There were lots of times she wanted to experiment, like any curious teenager, but she could never bring herself to act on her own desires. She was too scared that her mother might really do something drastic if she wavered from her maternal path. So Amy convinced herself that her mother's way was the right one, and she lived for years being the good, dutiful daughter.

Leslie, the younger of the two, was constantly outraged at her mother for saying those kinds of things to her and her sister. She was not going to let anybody tell her how to live her life. Whatever her mother wanted, Leslie defied her by doing the opposite. She was promiscuous because her mother wanted her to "save herself for marriage." She did drugs and alcohol because her mother looked down on anybody who so indulged. For years, Leslie was always angry about something and didn't understand why she was so miserable.

All too often, a potentially good, growing relationship will get bogged down when one person isn't open and honest about some painful emotion they are feeling. That person will often attempt to use guilt to get their partner to comply with their demands, rather than deal honestly with what is upsetting them. Of course, they are just acting out drama scenes with the appropriate lines that they observed and learned while growing up.

What can we do if we were raised to lay guilt trips rather than communicate honestly about our pain? What can we do if our friends or family try to relate to us with "guilt trips"?

First of all, we need to understand our behavior. What we do or don't do has an effect on those close to us. Some therapies talk about "you do your thing and I'll do mine." Others might have you focus only on your thoughts, feelings, decisions and actions, as if your life is a separate, insulated experience. I don't agree with this thinking. If we want meaningful, connected, long-term relationships, then we do need to take our friends and family and their thoughts and feelings into consideration. The key here is how to balance the consideration and thoughtfulness without sacrificing your own dreams and goals. Finding this balance is definitely possible.

Here are some helpful suggestions to assist you as you heal your life from the effects of guilt:

- Think about something you felt horribly guilty about in the past, or behavior in general that you know is wrong, such as killing, burning buildings down, etc. Try to get in touch with the old emotions from the incident in the past or the feelings you would have if you performed one of those crimes. This feeling of remorse has a physical component. Look in the mirror and notice your body posture, your facial expression. This is how you look when you feel guilty.
- Think of any non-violent dreams and goals that you have. (If you have any dreams and goals that are violent, it's a clear statement of how your life is being run by your distress and unhealed pains and wounds from the past). Think of how thrilled and delighted you would be if those goals came were achieved. Look in the mirror again, this time noticing your facial expressions and body postures.
- Work toward becoming keenly aware of the two different attitudes, along with the physical features and the thoughts that are associated with both. Then do your best everyday to focus your life toward the attitude that may bring you success and satisfaction and away from the attitude that will

likely lead you to failure and discontent.

- Ask yourself if you are giving in to some behavior that will eventually deplete your immune system as well as compromise your spirit.

- Some of us will feel guilt no matter what we do or don't do. In this case, do what you know is the right thing and allow yourself to feel the guilty feelings that are bound to arise. If you're going to feel guilty, you might as well do the right thing. Here's a place where you can use your intelligence to act rationally in spite of irrational feelings. This is also the place where you may get a chance to release some long-held emotional toxins. It's a good sign if tears or trembling begin to surface.

CHAPTER 7: Worry

∾∾∾

Lots of people have chronic nightmares of being chased by some horrible monster who is gaining on them with every step and is just about to catch them and eat them for dinner. The monster appears to be very mean and powerful and big, but in many cases it's just some feeling that the dreamer does not want to face.

If you turn and face the feeling with a willingness to release the emotional toxins that are bound to surface, you'll actually be pulling the plug on the power source of the painful emotion. This process of "making friends with the feeling" is directly connected to the reclaiming of your own power, rather than remaining powerless and being held hostage by it.

Attempting to face our fears is easier said than done, but in the long run we're much better off having done that. If we keep running from them, the tension has got to keep building. Eventually this avoidance can cause a chain reaction of events which ultimately can lead to our worst nightmares coming true—a self-fulfilling prophecy. Facing our fears, no matter how scary, often frees our lives from fear's hold over us.

A while back one night, I went to sleep at about 11 p.m. and woke up at 10 the next morning. Sleeping that long and getting up that late was a rare event for me. For years I have struggled with sleep, regularly waking up at 5 in the morning and not feeling well-rested. Over the years I have spent many counseling sessions where I did my best to release the emotional toxins that constantly came up for me, directly caused by my battle with sleep. Releasing these toxins helped me think more flexibly about my sleep dilemma, but it did not completely eliminate the problem.

So, what was the first thing I did when I realized that I slept for eleven hours? Instead of enjoying the moment, I immediately started to worry about myself. The internal warnings that went off were "Uh-oh, something must be really wrong with me." "Sleeping so long could be a sign of depression," along with "Maybe I have some disease that my body is fighting." But I had enough awareness in that moment to burst out laughing, realizing that my concern about getting enough sleep had been running completely out of control. It had grown into an irrational pattern of worry. The worry pattern was targeted on my unusual occurance of a long night's sleep, and ran rampant given the chance. It just didn't matter to the pattern. Its job was to get me to worry and it was going to do that.

Seeing this pattern so clearly was just like pulling the curtain on the Wizard of Oz, revealing a little man pushing and pulling a few levers and buttons. The jig was up. The pattern was exposed as if it were a totally separate entity that had been glommed onto my brain for a very long time. It immediately lost its power over me as if someone had pulled the plug. The clarity and tranquility I experienced were amazing.

In the world of counseling, we've learned that every distress pattern, including worry, has three major qualities: it confuses us, it makes us forget reality, and it persists. It's like a parasitic glob of gook that clings to our brains, distorting our perception of the world and causing us to alter our behavior. It has no intelligence of its own and cannot be reasoned with. This is an important point. You will never be able to convince the pattern to self-destruct. It has survived by leeching energy from the person that it is attached to and it will do whatever it can to stay "alive." Attempts to reason with any pattern will always be futile and are a waste of time and energy.

However, the pattern's irrational behavior can be interrupted, the negative internal recordings can be contradicted, and the emotional toxins that fuel the pattern can be released. This is the only successful way that I'm aware of to completely eliminate the power and destructive influence of the distress pattern.

A little history. My mother's father died rather suddenly from tuberculosis when she was twelve. She was shocked and terrified to have lost the man she had loved so much. When I was born, my mother focused her love on me, and along with that love came her unconscious terror of losing me to some dreaded disease. Guess what distress pattern I internalized? I became convinced that my health and well being were constantly in jeopardy. As a child, I was innocent and vulnerable, with no information about the world other than what I received from my parents. Looking back, I know that I felt or intuited her fear, which was frequently targeted at my body. So, the result was that I have been worrying about my health, on some level, as long as I can remember. Influencing my ability to sleep has been one of the most effective ways the pattern has infiltrated my being and altered my behavior. My mother's behavior was also affected by her pattern. Besides worrying about my health, she struggled with sleep her whole life.

We know that any distress recordings that are not held up to the light, thoroughly examined and questioned, become part of our belief system. Once we believe them as reality, we become enslaved by their distorted view of the world and methodically go about altering our behavior based on the misinformation. The irrational behavior supports and reinforces the distorted perception and mis-information. For example, the more I worried about not getting a good night's sleep, the more difficulty I had with sleeping.

People who worry are people who are scared and are often not aware of how frightened they really are. There are many reasons for fear to arise, but, in general, people who worry usually get scared because they are not able to be in control of a situation. This lack of control, along with their inability to trust in life, which is just an expression of some earlier hurt that did not get healed, leaves them in a state of anxiety or nervousness. In my case, the worry pattern that took over for me and my good thinking wanted to watch over my body when I was sleeping, just to make sure nothing went wrong. This strange behavior was directly related to the internaliz-ing of my mother's distresses due to her father's sudden illness and subsequent death.

If my mother had had an aware counselor or friend to help her grieve the loss of her father, while giving her rational, useful infor-mation about her father's death and its effect on her life back then, she likely would not have had the worry pattern to pass on to me. Furthermore, if I had had an aware counselor or friend to help me differentiate between my mother's distress and the reality about my body, I would never have internalized the pattern.

Since neither my mother nor I had aware counselors to help us out of the muck, it was now my job to dismantle the pattern. My revelation of "seeing" the worry pattern as non-reality was a won-derful gift, but it did not eliminate the pattern. It only defused it temporarily. Too often in the world of healing, people become aware, but still go on functioning irrationally due to a lack of importance given to the process of releasing the emotional toxins. My job from now on is to eliminate whatever remaining distress recordings and emotional toxins might be in the way of trusting my body, to learn and understand the difference between thinking well about my body and worrying about it, and, whenever I find myself worrying, to acknowledge that I am scared and need to release some fear.

When we free ourselves from the fear connected to worrying about something, we become more able to think flexibly about the situation—whatever it may be. This is true on a personal level as well as a global level.

Here are some helpful hints that may assist you in your attempt to dismantle your pattern of worry.

- Observe yourself while worrying about something, then write down your concern on a piece of paper. If you're not aware of what you worry about, just ask your friends or family members. It's usually obvious to others. They should be able to give you accurate information about the areas where you have some nervous anxiety. Writing them down is a good tool that will help you remember. One of the qualities of a pattern of distress is its ability to get us to forget things.
- Worrying is a form of obsession, which is mostly behavior based on fear. If you expose the pattern, it will always lose a good portion of its power. So let's work toward exposing your pattern of worrying. Do your best to repeat all the parts of the pattern in front of a mirror or a trusted friend. Say the phrases out loud that are connected with the worrying pattern. Then add your specific kind of nervous tone that

almost always accompanies those phrases. With your growing awareness, attempt to make the facial expressions and
body postures that are associated with the worrying pattern.
Most of us have specific physical responses that go along
with the phrases and tones.

- Once you've got the phrase, tone, facial expression, and
body posture down, you'll probably start spontaneously
releasing some emotional toxins, tears, trembling, rage, or
laughter. Allow the feelings to flow for awhile. Toxins will be
released and your flexible thinking will eventually surface.
There is no time limit on this part of the process. Some anxieties will drip away in a few minutes, others may last for
months. Each person needs to respect his or her body's
process without judgment.

- You can do this on your own or with a friend. However, if the
releasing of old emotional toxins calls for more support, you
might join a support group or hire a counselor or therapist to
give you some temporary assistance with the healing.

- Work toward being able to differentiate between worrying
and thinking about things. Worrying is filled with nervous
anxiety and is a waste of time. Getting information about a
situation and then using that information to intelligently
make decisions will inevitably lead you toward a healthier
lifestyle.

CHAPTER 8: Blame

ന~ന~ന

The frustrated young woman was quietly eating dinner with her mother. Her food tasted a little bland and she looked around for some seasoning. Then, instead of saying "Would you please pass the salt?" she inadvertently blurted out, "I hate you and you've ruined my whole life."

It's very important for you to take responsibility for your thoughts, your feelings, your decisions, and your actions. Growth usually comes more smoothly and healing typically is more effective for those who take on an attitude of being responsible for their lives. Earlier conditioning often makes this hard for some of us. Years ago I came up with this little jingle that has helped me stay on track, "Responsibility/ it means so much to me/ to check myself to see/ if I blame others constantly."

Blaming others constantly is something that is done too often in our society. Everybody's blaming everybody else for everything that goes wrong, pointing fingers at someone for every mistake that is made. The "blame game" is unconsciously supported and encouraged by the legal system and the insurance businesses in our country. If you are "at fault" for an accident, the insurance companies raise your rates immediately. Because of this blame mentality, there is a strong tendency to shirk or avoid responsibility for mistakes.

Then there's the plight of the deeply deprived in our country, who turn to crime as a desperate attempt to "beat the system" that has them locked into such a difficult life. They know what they're doing is wrong, and they know that, if caught, they will be punished. But they blame society for their problems and commit crimes anyway, in a desperate attempt to avoid the constant pain and misery of their lives. For these people things usually get worse.

In this book I occasionally talk about the mistreatment I endured as a child, how I was unfairly blamed for so many things that went wrong and consistently beaten by my father. This set me up to play the blame game as a creative attempt to keep myself from being abused. Many children get blamed as I did, and then are unconsciously compelled to blame others constantly. They unwittingly follow a path that gets them caught up in refusing any responsibility for their lives. This is devastating to our children and to our children's future.

In general, there is a sequence to the integration of the patterned behavior. First, children get blamed way too much and are often punished severely. Then they almost always feel bad about themselves, resent the unfair results, and feel they have no power in righting the situation. Next, children will start the blame game: "It's not my fault. I didn't do it. Johnny did. It's his fault." This begins the wall of defensiveness and denial, a distorted attempt to creatively solve an impossible and unfair situation. Somewhere at this point in the cycle, children begin the rationalization process that results in them refusing to acknowledge, occasionally even to themselves, that they had some responsibility for events that took place. As this wall gets thicker, many children will take on a pattern of pretense, acting like everything is fine and there are no problems in their lives. These children either have rigid, frozen smiles on their faces, or they look continually spaced out, with very little ability to focus on anything. Those who don't go the pretense route usually are fearful and defensive about almost everything.

A while back, I went for a drive with a friend during a vacation break. It was late afternoon and we got stuck in traffic. I said, "I can't believe this traffic. What a drag."

"Excuse me for driving," she said, in a slightly hostile, very sarcastic voice. "This is the only road I could have taken."

I was surprised at her response, but continued to do some griping. "And the sun is shining right into my eyes," I said.

"Forgive me for living," she retorted defensively and in a huff. "I can't help it."

I was frustrated with the traffic and bothered by the sun's glare, but never blamed her for either. She, however, reacted as if I had. I stopped our conversation and thought about the pile of criticism and blame she must have endured as a child to be so defensive. She had been living a life completely caught up in defensiveness, which led her down a path where she rarely took any responsibility for herself and her actions. She was extremely overweight, continually unhappy with so many things, and was, as a result of the pattern, blaming others for what was wrong in her life. She was locked into an existence of blaming or being blamed. She couldn't relate in any other way.

I felt sad for her, remembering how it had been for me when my father blamed me for everything.

People who carry this kind of attitude can't be in relationships without having the blame stuff, sooner or later, rear its ugly head.

Couples who get caught up in blaming each other for difficulties in their relationship are, in effect, weaving a sticky web that will eventually strangle both people and sabotage any hope of a successful partnership. Obviously, there are other, healthier options. If something is not going well in the relationship, it is necessary for both partners to take responsibility for the difficulty. "We have a problem" or "I have a problem" is much more workable than "You have a problem." Remember, consistently pointing out someone's defects usually evokes anger and defensiveness, and rarely results in any positive change.

Other options that can be used to defuse the blame game:

- "I have a problem and I want you to help me think about it."
- "Whenever you do (blank), it makes me feel (blank)."
- "How can we, together, come up with a solution to this problem?"
- "Let's not blame each other or find fault with each other here, let's ..."

When we choose to blame, we're giving up our power on an emotional level. We have the potential power to figure out healthy, elegant solutions to most difficulties and struggles. It's fascinating to me to see so many people choosing behavior that discourages clear thinking and powerful action. This, albeit very sad, is not the fault of the people who are caught in this behavior. Everybody is doing the best they are capable of doing, taking everything into consideration. Criticism of people who are functioning irrationally almost never helps the situation, and more often than not adds more distress to an already distressing predicament.

Are you in charge of your life? Do you want to be more in

charge of it? For most of us, the quickest, most effective way to be more in charge of our lives is to interrupt any time we catch ourselves in the blame game. The questions need to shift from "Who's to blame?" and "Whose fault is it?" to "What needs to happen here to get things back on track?" and "What can I do to help bring healing and harmony to this situation?" Taking these more useful attitudes will likely bring some emotional toxins to the surface. Releasing them rather than suppressing them will assist you in the shifting of your attitudes.

Remember, every day is new and you are capable of making a fresh start. You have the potential every day of refusing the pull to act out the same old self-defeating patterns of behavior that have made your life difficult and miserable. It may take some time to correct a pattern of blame, but it is completely possible to end the acting out of old patterns. In fact, it's completely possible to shift your attitudes and perceptions away from the old, distressing stuff and toward more interesting and rewarding attitudes and perceptions. If it's true that we are wired, as human beings, to live out our existence on the planet according to what we believe in, then why not set up our belief systems to insure that our lives will go well? If you believe in something negative about yourself or your friends or family, I want you to question that belief. You have the power to choose what you believe in. Don't forget this!

Three men went to the hospital and were all told by their doctors that they had a terminal form of cancer and would only live another six months. The first guy went out of control with panic, had a heart attack right there on the spot, and died. The second took the information "like a man" and methodically took care of business over the next six months, and then died. The third guy refused to believe the prognosis. He went to a few other doctors until he found a doctor who was willing to work with him on setting up a program for healing his body from the illness. He's still alive and doing fine!

CHAPTER 9: Pretense

When I was very young I used to play pretending games with my friends. We'd pretend to be cowboys and indians, swashbuckling pirates searching for treasure, jet fighter pilots, kings and princes. All this play was innocent and fun.

As I got older I pretended to be strong when I was too scared to show anybody how weak I felt. I remember pretending to be sick to get some attention from my mother, who often ignored me, pretending to be hurt or exhausted to get out of doing chores, pretending to be sleeping so I wouldn't get caught with my transistor under my pillow, pretending to know something rather than admit ignorance to friends.

This kind of pretending started out as an innocent attempt to get my needs met as a child, but eventually turned into a part of my personality. I got the message loud and clear from my parents, my friends, and the community I lived in that most of my spontaneous and natural thoughts, feelings, and actions were not acceptable. I had to pretend to think, feel, and act in certain "more appropriate" ways or I'd be punished or at least ignored.

The pattern of pretending to be different than who I really was eventually took on a life of its own. I found myself compelled to exaggerate all the time. If I got an eighty on an exam, I told friends that I got an eighty-five. If I bowled a score of one-fifty, I had to tell people I bowled one-sixty. I exaggerated about my height, my weight, how much weight I could lift, and how much money I had. The truth was never acceptable in my mind. The message that I bought completely was that I was not enough, therefore I had to prove to everybody that I was more. Then, maybe, I would be recognized and appreciated.

I carried that pretentious behavior for many years, all as a distorted attempt to get attention, recognition, and acceptance from friends and family. The truth was that no matter how much recognition I did receive from them, it never felt like enough for me. I was not accepting of myself. I had believed the original invalidating criticisms were true about me. I believed that I was not enough and was never able to relax and accept myself for who I was. I always wanted to be more.

Thanks to my years of counseling work, I've cleansed my system of this toxic behavior. On occasion I get urges to exaggerate, but I do pretty well at resisting them. Looking back, one of the scariest parts of the pretentious behavior was that for a long time I didn't know the difference between the real me and the pretentious me. I lost my ability to separate the two, and thus lost connection with myself.

That's exactly what pretentious behavior can do to people. It's toxic.

Dramatizing

Dramatizing, like a half-sibling to pretense, originates in similar ways, but looks a little different. As children, many of us felt neglected, especially when we were hurting, and really needed at least one parent to show he or she cared. Too often our natural pleas for loving attention fell on deaf ears. A natural reaction to this was to make noise for that cherished attention. Lots of us did get noticed more when we made more noise, so, as a survival decision, we learned to make more noise when we needed to be cared for. "The squeaky wheel always gets the grease" was the kind of statement that reinforced our decisions to dramatize.

Dramatizing takes two forms. Both are usually reactions to some incident of hurt. One form of dramatizing appears as an over-exaggeration of the pain received from any hurtful incident. The other form appears as held-in resentment and withdrawal. Both are unconscious attempts to get attention from parents or friends by acting out a drama scene. The sad part about dramatizing is that even when you get attention from someone, it's not very satisfying. You know, on some level, that the attention you get usually is for the drama scene, not really for you.

When times get difficult, we all have a tendency to get caught up in the drama of the difficulty. This always feeds the negativity and is toxic to the body as well. Dramatizing must be interrupted. It's not useful, it causes more damage, and it plays right into a phony kind of pretentiousness. Let me give you an example.

Phrases like "I'm sick and tired of (whatever the difficulty is)" and "my (difficulty) is killing me" are fuel for our irrational distresses and negative behaviors. These normally acceptable phrases are energy zappers and exaggerate negative situations. In fact, it's not a coincidence that many people who consistently use the phrase "I'm sick and tired of..." are often physically ill and constantly exhausted. A more connected and less toxic phrase would be "I'm so angry about..." or "I'm so frustrated about ..." These phrases are honest and more emotionally connected, with much less drama, pretense or exaggeration. These are much healthier ways of responding to difficulties in that they directly state feelings. Dramatizing, though, merely tends to burden our immune systems and deplete our energy.

The same is true about the phrase "This is killing me" or any variation of the same. This is pure pretense and drama. Unless someone is poisoning you, putting a knife through your heart, or pulling the trigger to a loaded gun pointed directly at your head, nothing about the situation is actually "killing" you, in spite of the painful emotions that you might be feeling. Ironically, your dramatic phrase, originally an attempt for attention and a chance to heal, is giving the message, over and over again, to your subconscious that you are being killed. This is destructive to your well-being, once again burdening your immune system and depleting your energy. A more appropriate, more honest, and less toxic phrase would be "This is really upsetting me" or "This is very frustrating to me." These phrases are more honest, less dramatic, and will not deplete your energy.

It appears to me that the behavioral patterns of dramatization and pretentiousness become cemented into one's personality because of an accompanying emotional parasite known as denial. Many people who have received effective help and have gone on to grow usually have been aware of their difficulties and have reached out for help. It's very challenging to assist a person out of a destructive pattern of behavior if he won't admit he has a problem in the first place. There's a T-shirt that accentuates the absurdity of denial. It says "I don't have a drinking problem. I drink, I get drunk,

I fall flat on my face. No problem."

If you are interested in cleansing your system of the toxins of pretense, dramatization, and denial:

- Watch your behavior over the next few days and make a note of one or two places where you exaggerate the truth or where you feel compelled to be a little dramatic. Most of us flip into varying degrees of pretentiousness or dramatization on occasion.
- Admit to yourself in no uncertain terms that you do dramatize or act pretentious on occasion. Admitting this to yourself will take the air out of any pull to give in to denial. Look in a mirror and admit it. Say it out loud so you can hear yourself owning up to yourself. There is no need to feel like you should punish or condemn yourself in any way. That is useless and counter-productive to the healing process.
- Observe family members—parents, siblings, and children—to see if any of them have similar patterns of behavior. Often we learn this behavior from loved ones, unconsciously taking on pieces of their personalities. If you notice similar behavior, observe what happens to their faces and their postures when they are dramatizing or pretentious. Any similarities to the way you act? Also check out their phrases and inflections of tone. You might hear the same things that you're used to saying. Families commonly use the same expressions, having learned them from the same source.
- Watch other people, especially children. They are usually more open and expressive with their pretense and dramas. Work toward being able to see the difference between honest human responses to life and reactions of drama and pretense.

- If you choose to stop your own dramatizing or pretentious behavior you must prepare yourself for the surfacing of emotional toxins. The toxins will surface for emotional cleansing through tears, trembling, rage, or laughter. You can choose to release whatever emotions arise on your own, if appropriate, or seek out a friend, counselor, or support group to insure safety while releasing. The cleansing will be effective with the release of emotional toxins. Whenever you interrupt your own toxic behavior of any kind, emotional toxins will spontaneously surface to be cleansed from your system. As you release these toxins, the pull to act out the toxic behavior diminishes.

- Always appreciate yourself for making the decision to grow away from toxic behavior and toward a more healthy human connection with yourself and others.

CHAPTER 10: Addictions
ↄↄↄ

If you haven't worked out your issues regarding pretense, you're not going to be able to admit that you have any addictions.

Most of us are born into this world free of addictions. As the years of childhood pass, we experience lots of pleasure and pain. If our natural healing processes of crying, trembling, laughing, etc., are cut off or inhibited, we lose our ability to keep our bodies clean from the build-up of emotional toxins. As these deposits of toxins increase, our ability to receive and give love gets distorted. Our ability to communicate and cooperate with others gets harder and harder, and our ability to think flexibly is replaced by a tough and rigid set of beliefs about our world. The more the emotional toxins build up from additional hurtful experiences, the more they try to ooze out at any opportunity. This causes even more anxiety because in our society many of us are not comfortable about showing others that we are in pain. So, as a desperate attempt to avoid showing to others how much pain we're in, we scramble to find something that will take us away from feeling the pain, something that will move us more toward "feeling good."

At this point we are totally vulnerable to some addictive substance or some addictive behavior. Drugs or alcohol will temporarily move us from pain to pleasure, or at least to an altered state where we are temporarily free from constant pain. But when the effects of the drug or alcohol wear off, we all know we're left feeling the same emotional pain as before, along with physical pain caused by the toxins from the drug or the alcohol. Now, we start believing the only thing we can do to avoid all these horrible feelings is to do more of the drug or alcohol. Thus we fall into the typical pattern that takes place when our bodies become addicted. We get so lost and disconnected that we actually believe that the best thing we can do for our situation is to "have another drink." The addiction has permeated our thinking and we're no longer capable of rational, healthy decisions.

Alcohol and drugs tend to be seen as the worst substances to be addicted to. Their effect on the body is devastating and some people who are addicted even have a strong tendency toward committing crimes and acting violently toward others. Caffeine and nicotine are addictive substances with less dramatic behavioral distortions, but are also toxic to the body. Sugar, overeating, gambling, and compulsive sex are addictions that can also be severely dehumanizing. If you free your body from addictive substances, you will have an excellent chance of full recovery of your humanity, the possibility of recovering a healthy lifestyle, and the opportunity to develop healthy, loving relationships.

There have been lots of books written about freeing oneself from the effects of addictions. I think they are well-meaning books that have excellent ideas and good steps to follow in the pursuit of an addiction-free life. I'm sure these books can be quite useful, and I encourage anyone who sincerely wants to clean up an addiction to read these books and use the support groups that are available.

However, there are a few places of confusion.

A couple of years ago, I sat in on a few Alcoholics Anonymous meetings with some friends who had been trying to break their addictions. I saw lots of good people doing their best to support each other away from drinking. They all really wanted to stop having their lives ruined by the addiction and they all sincerely wanted to be supportive to others at the meetings. It was impressive and the results seemed to be very good to me. But there were a couple of places where I thought they were lacking information.

They were not drinking alcohol, which was great, but almost everyone at the meetings had a cigarette in one hand and a cup of coffee in the other. The addictive pull still held them captive. They had unconsciously gone from alcohol to caffeine and nicotine. They still needed something to alter their feelings because they still did not know what to do with the stored-up tension from the emotional toxins.

Were they to stop the cigarettes and coffee too, their bodies would inevitably begin the process of purging emotional toxins. This would happen spontaneously on a physical level, but once again the mind would be confused and probably would figure out a way to inhibit the body's healing process. Until the emotional toxins are cleaned out of the body, however, the person is held hostage by the unreleased feelings. Avoiding the painful emotions will always lead you back toward some addiction. Keep the feelings inhibited, and you have a game of discipline and will power, which can be exhausting and often ends in failure. Release the emotional toxins, and you free the body permanently of the irrational desire to be numb or altered in some way as a means of escape.

It's important to remember that you are good no matter how bad you feel at any moment. Once you make the decision to stop the irrational behavior, you give your body permission to release the stored-up toxic emotional tension. If you can do this, there is absolutely no need to escape. Remember, the emotions that need to come out are the same ones that you've always wanted to get out, even when you were a child. They are painful. Since we've been conditioned to identify with what we are feeling (for example, "I feel bad, therefore I am bad"), the last thing we want to feel are these painful emotions. But if you don't get these painful feelings out, they become emotional toxins and they can slowly destroy your life.

Years ago, I had a very determined client who stopped smoking in spite of her two-pack-a-day addiction. She then proceeded to cry and shake for the better part of a month. Cory felt terrible almost all the time during that period, but was determined to free herself from the addiction. She was blessed to have lots of friends and counselors in her life who were relaxed with her shaking and crying. They frequently held her and gave her loving attention when she needed it, never slipping into confusion about her body's releases. During the month, Cory kept talking about how bad she felt and how bad she felt about herself. This was her healing process at work. Cory needed to get out all the negative recordings that she had believed about herself for years. As long as she had people around her who believed in her and not in the negative recordings in her head or the painful emotions she was releasing, she was able to continue the purging. After the month, she was completely free of the addiction as well as being completely free of the desire to be run by some addiction. She didn't have to "keep it together" anymore. The desire for a smoke was gone and so were years of her feeling bad about herself. With all the emotional toxins finally out of her system, the natural healing process helped her reclaim the inherent knowledge that she is and always was a good person. She also realized that sometimes she felt bad, but that didn't mean that she was bad.

It was beautiful to watch this woman, previously held down by the addiction of cigarette smoking, reclaim her love of herself, her children, and her whole life.

Once again, the key pieces are to always remember that you are good no matter what you are feeling at any moment, and to understand and be at peace with the body's natural ability to heal itself through crying, shaking, etc. It's also very important to be sweet to yourself when you're releasing pent-up emotions and to refuse any pull to invalidate or judge yourself negatively. The truth is that if you've taken on the challenge of freeing yourself from some addiction, you have guts and deserve to have lots of support to help you on your path toward health. Likewise, if you are supporting friends through their attempt at freeing themselves from some addiction, you, too, deserve lots of cheers as well as support. It might be difficult for your friends to be thoughtful about you while they battle their addictions, but when their battles are over, it's likely they'll be grateful and totally amazed that you hung in there with them.

CHAPTER 11: Powerlessness
∾∾∾

Nine-year-old Josie came home from school and threw her books down on the living room floor. "Betsy and Ellen went roller skating and didn't invite me," she said, with tears welling up in her eyes. Her mother just listened. "But I don't care," Josie continued, "because I hate them and I wouldn't ever want to be seen with them."

"But you and Betsy have been good friends for two years," her mother responded.

"I don't care about Betsy anymore and I never really liked her anyway."

Powerlessness affects many of us daily and has had a devastating effect on our lives since we were children. It's incredibly toxic to believe that there is nothing we can do to stop mistreatment by others or correct horrible conditions in society. It's exhausting and debilitating to think that we are helpless to get ourselves out of victim roles or unhealthy situations. This type of toxic attitude leads to a sense of hopelessness and apathy, with many people turning toward drugs, alcohol, crime, and other self-destructive behavior.

A few years ago, I heard of a teenage couple who committed suicide together rather than accept the rigid control of their parents. Two fifteen-year-olds, a Chinese girl and an American boy, fell in love and wanted to get married. Both sets of parents not only wholeheartedly rejected their marriage plans, but refused to allow them to even see each other anymore. The teenage lovers were devastated. They loved each other and desperately wanted to figure out a way to be together. They were tormented by knowing the anguish their parents felt. Their friends were not supportive either, ridiculing and harassing them. They were in pain and felt completely alone. They hated being intimidated and controlled by everyone and made a pact with each other to never give in. They were deeply hurt, very angry, and terrified about the increasing pressure of the situation. They couldn't deal anymore with rebelling, but they couldn't bear to give in and not be together. In their tortured minds there was only one thing to do to escape the insanity—to commit suicide and be together in death.

This is a good example of what happens to us when we give in to powerlessness. Neither one of them ever thought about getting on a bus and leaving town to pursue a happy life together somewhere else. Their best "thinking" was to kill themselves to escape the pain and struggle.

This was obviously an extreme case, but nevertheless this is how the toxicity of powerlessness can distort our thinking and lead us to even more toxic decisions. However, it doesn't have to be this way.

I remember as a teenager watching an ongoing scene between two friends of mine. I was fascinated with it, but didn't know why at the time. Now I understand. I was observing a classic case of the events that happen between perpetrator and victim, along with seeing the possibilities that can happen when victims receive healthy support from caring friends.

Stanley was a tall thirteen-year-old with a medium build. His father had beaten him frequently when he was younger, and Stanley had developed a stutter whenever he spoke. He was a nice guy, but always appeared to be scared.

Jerry, also thirteen, was short, stocky, and sharp-witted, with a bit of a chip on his shoulder. He used to yell at people, often for no reason, ordering them around, and seemed to always expect to get his way.

Jerry used to constantly harass Stanley, mimicking his stutter and making him feel bad about himself. Jerry would humiliate Stanley in front of people, almost as an enjoyable way to pass the time. On occasion, when Stanley would attempt to defend himself with some shaky verbal comebacks, Jerry would get pissed off and start punching him. Stanley would either plead for Jerry to stop or he'd run away.

Stanley had two other friends, Harris, 14, and Jackie, 16, who were brothers. They were disgusted with watching Stanley's abuse, and the way he allowed Jerry to dominate him. So they made a decision to help. All they did, however, was to help Stanley with his confidence, something he was sorely lacking. They pointed out to Stanley that he was bigger and stronger than Jerry, and that he could respond differently to Jerry's abusive ways. In fact, he could fight back if he had to.

It took time. For weeks and weeks the brothers encouraged Stanley to give up the victim role and to believe in himself.

Then one day, a couple of months later, Jerry began to mess with Stanley again. But this time the results were different. Stanley didn't back down. Though his body was trembling with fear and his lips stuttering so much he could hardly speak, he took a stand.

"L-l-l-leave m-me alone, J-Jerry. I'm not gonna t-take your crap anymore," he said cautiously and with hesitation.

Jerry was surprised, then started yelling louder and began hitting Stanley. Stanley backed up, winced a little, and then made fists and started hitting Jerry back. One punch hurt Jerry and he stumbled to the ground. Jerry was totally stunned and looked confused and tentative, but got up and began to throw punches wildly in an attempt to reclaim his dominating role. Stanley, still trembling, kept looking right at Jerry, ducked a few times, and then hit Jerry again. Jerry went down. Jerry looked up at Stanley with a new respect, mumbled some curse words, but did not do anything else.

Jerry's domination of Stanley was over. He never attempted to humiliate or hurt him again. Stanley, on the other hand, gained a world of confidence from the episode. He carried that confidence through the remaining years that I knew him.

Harris and Jackie were great friends to Stanley. They did not dominate Jerry the way that Jerry had been dominating Stanley. Together they could have easily beaten up Jerry in "support" of their friend. But they did something much better. They helped Stanley gain confidence in himself by expressing to him what they knew was true about Stanley. They continually encouraged him to take a stand and not allow the old fear and powerless feelings to keep him victimized. They believed in him when he didn't believe in himself, and it made the difference.

Powerlessness is rooted in fear and misinformation. We've all been tricked into believing lots of things about ourselves and our world that aren't true. We all have more power than we know. We have the power to change our attitudes about ourselves; we can achieve healthy, meaningful lives. Most people are capable of making powerful changes, but just like achieving anything worthwhile, it takes a sincere commitment and work.

The work we do to help ourselves heal and enjoy better lives, along with the commitment we make to sustain this work over a period of time, seems to be directly proportional to the love we have for ourselves. Here's a story I heard at a workshop from a woman who made this kind of commitment to herself and reaped the rewards.

Sherry, a thirty-year-old woman who had lived in Hawaii, told me that she had struggled with all sorts of physical and emotional problems from having been raped years ago on three separate occasions. She had carried tons of fear, had been deeply insecure, and had a belief that only death would save her from her life of misery.

She knew, though, deeply hidden underneath the pain and anger, that she was a good person, and thus refused to give up on herself or her life. She got involved in counseling, learned some important tools to help her with her healing, and began to chip away at the layers of distress in an attempt to piece her life back together. She said she worked responsibly for a couple of years, slowly reclaiming her confidence. As she released old emotional toxins from the times she had been victimized, she began to think more powerfully and more flexibly.

Sherry told me that she took a karate class to tune up her body and to insure herself that she would never again fall into being a helpless victim. She gained confidence in herself, getting pretty skilled in the techniques, but never thought she'd need to use them in real life.

Months later, late one night while she was walking home, a man sprang out of the woods, grabbed her, and threw her down on the ground. It was the old rape scene repeating once again, and a flood of memories from the past flashed through her mind. As the man got closer, she felt all the old fear and panic as her muscles momentarily went limp. But she kept thinking, and in the next instant she realized that she had choices. She did not have to play out the same old scenario. When he lunged at her, she kicked him, catching him completely off guard. She gave another two kicks to his body as he came at her for a second time, entirely thwarting his efforts.

Then something new happened for her, she said. She saw his face and noticed that he was just as scared as she was. Sherry said they looked at each other for a second or two and then the man decided to leave her alone. He turned, looked around, then started jogging away. Sherry, pumped with adrenalin and soaring with confidence, said she was feeling very angry and wanted the man to be punished for his actions. She got up and started chasing him down the road. "I wouldn't have known what to do with him if I had actually caught him," she said. "But it just felt good to chase him."

He turned around, saw her coming and began to run away, even faster than before. "The roles were reversed for a change," she said, proudly recounting this part of the story. Sherry said that she followed him for six blocks before letting go of the chase. She hoped she scared the guy enough to prevent him from ever attempting to rape another woman. She said she felt exhilarated while chasing him, and felt great about herself and how far she had come in reclaiming her female body, her power, and her pride.

Reclaiming power is not just about developing physical strength. It's about believing in yourself and refusing any situations that keep you locked in a victim role. If someone has a gun pointed at your head and he tells you to eat garbage, you may need to make a decision to temporarily comply with his demand, but you never have to give in to accept a permanent victim personality. So, in the moment you eat the garbage, then wait until you can either figure out a way to get the gun out of his hands or how to get yourself away from the situation.

The classic prisoner of war is set free after five or so years in captivity. He is heralded as a hero for not having complied with the enemy. His ability to maintain his clear thinking remains intact, in spite of the incredibly stressful conditions.

When we give in to powerlessness we are, in a psychological sense, prisoners of war. Many people give in to the belief that there is nothing they can do to improve their situation or the situation of their community or country. This is not true, however if powerless thinking permeates the mind, it becomes part of the person's belief system. Then powerlessness wins, apathy takes over, and the free-thinking human being loses.

On the other hand, when you refuse powerless thoughts and reclaim a strong belief in your thinking, your ability to reach goals and accomplish things will be greatly enhanced. Sooner or later in your life you will reap the rewards from having not given in to powerlessness.

At this point I'd like you to ask yourself a few questions.

- Where have I given into powerlessness and how does this kind of thinking limit my life?
- Who told me I had those limits and why did I believe them?
- Am I willing to explore the possibility that this information about me is not true now and never was?
- What if I made the decision right now to not respect those powerless thoughts ever again?
- What would I immediately start to improve or change in my life, the lives of my friends, my family, and my community?

- What powerless thoughts might attempt to get in my way?
- Do I have the determination and perseverance to continually refuse to respect those powerless thoughts and actually see to it that my life goes well?

Hillel, a well-respected rabbi from the past, was recognized for his famous quote, "If I am not for myself, then who will be? If I am only for myself, then what am I? If not now...when?"

It's your life. They're your thoughts. You get to choose!

PART 2: The Cleansers

In Part 1 we discussed the emotional toxins that have built up in our bodies from years of unhealed wounds from the past, and the irrational, disconnected, misguided perspectives and accompanying behavior that almost always leads us to isolation and pain. All too often in the world of psychology we examine and analyze our dysfunctions, but are still left with frustration and confusion when we find ourselves continuing with the irrational behavior. Now that we have become aware of the toxins and their destructive power, we need to learn how to actually free our minds and bodies from the compulsion to continue to feed negativity. In Part 2 we will discuss the cleansers—the human being's natural healing processes that lead to emotional and physical health and well-being as well as mental clarity and spiritual growth.

As you reclaim the ability to be at peace with your own natural healing process, your ability to interrupt toxic behavior will grow in strength. Remember, anytime you interrupt toxic actions or attitudes you open the door to healing. However, when you interrupt toxic conditioning you must be willing to handle the emotional toxins that are sure to surface. Understanding the potency of the cleansers and skillfully integrating them into your life will give you the tools needed for transitioning with success.

CHAPTER 1: Tears
∿∿∿

"My tears are like precious jewels. Treat them with honor and respect, as you would rubies and diamonds."

We have been trained to believe that when we are crying, we are hurting and in some form of pain. This is only half the story. We cry when something upsets us. This is something that comes naturally to all of us. We are releasing the emotional tension from whatever has upset us, but we are also unconsciously engaging our own natural healing mechanism in an attempt to free ourselves from the distress that has invaded our system.

Tears are the outward sign of the healing process at work. True, you are in some form of pain, but the act of crying and the flow of tears are the body's natural cleansing process.

This is not unlike other forms of cleansing and purifying that the body does naturally. Any foreign or toxic substance that finds its way into the body almost immediately comes in contact with some variation of the body's defense system. The body will do whatever it can to render the toxic substance harmless and move it out.

This is a fascinating process to observe, and is true on an emotional level as well as on a physical one.

Our society has gone completely astray in the understanding of this beautiful healing process. We have erroneously assumed that if we get someone to stop crying, they will stop hurting. The opposite is true. When we interfere with the natural healing process, in effect we stop the person from healing.

If you observe little children who, in general, have not had their natural healing processes interfered with yet, you will see them experience a hurt, immediately seek out a safe and trusted loved one, run to them, and shed some tears, instantly attempting to heal on the spot. When a child is given the relaxed attention, physical warmth, and safety needed, he or she will release the tension from the hurt, and the healing will come to a natural completion. When this occurs, the child usually will go back to their activity with no emotional wounds from the hurt experience.

I think a confusing piece here is that we've seen people reach that place of completion, when the tears end and the smile comes back on their faces. When we care about someone, it brings up painful feelings in us to see them hurting. So, it makes sense that we would want to help them reach that place of completion, where their smile slowly reappears and life looks good again. The problem seems to arise in the timing. We often get anxious and impatient with the length of time someone needs to shed tears before they reach that natural ending place. With good intentions, we try to speed up the process rather than relax and allow the process to take its natural course. This innocent attempt to help is often exactly what interrupts the healing process and stops the true healing.

Can you remember a time when you felt uncomfortable and impatient when a good friend was crying? Do you remember any times when your tears were prematurely interrupted by a close friend? Most of us have probably had some caring friend or relative interrupt our own crying in just this very way. Each of us has undoubtedly interrupted a good friend in the same way. None of us ever knew we were obstructing the healing processes at work.

Healing works best when we are allowed to release the emotional tension from the hurtful experience. Crying and tears are the outward indications of one form of this healing process taking place.

Once, in a counseling session, I recalled a time in college when I was awakened by my roommate in the middle of the night. He woke me up because I was having a bad dream. He told me that I was sobbing out loud and calling out my old girlfriend's name. I remembered feeling so embarrassed to be caught with tears rolling down my face. I was so controlled during my waking hours back then that I hadn't even realized how much I had missed my old girlfriend.

I remember feeling delighted in that session, realizing that in spite of all the suppression of emotions acquired from my early conditioning, my body had creatively persisted in finding ways to do its best to heal itself.

Many years later I went to an intense counseling workshop where I learned more about the release of tears and the healing process. For one overwhelming week I was whisked from one event to another. My brain barely kept pace with the changes I was experiencing, the awareness I was developing, and the dozens of brilliant and loving men and women I was meeting. The quality of attention from individuals as well as from the workshop as a whole was simply astounding. The incredible stories of hurtful experiences that I heard from men and women I had just met and the counseling sessions I witnessed were powerful, full of intense emotional releases that truly held me in awe. I was witnessing good people all around me taking courageous steps to free themselves from the effects of old wounds from the past.

One evening the leader of the workshop counseled a woman on being raped, a horrible experience that she had gone through a couple of years before. I knew women were being raped in the world, but I had never thought twice about it. All I knew was that I wasn't raping anybody so it wasn't my concern. The woman started telling the story, with all the details of how she was victimized, along with her raging, shaking, and grieving about the terror, mistreatment, and loss of her dignity. I remember being totally stunned. I cried buckets of tears as she took all of us through the horror, and as my awareness grew regarding the oppression of women in our society, I swore that I would do everything I could to support and empower women against such outrageous acts of violence. The workshop accelerated my learning and growing by leaps and bounds. I remember feeling like it was a utopia to me, all the magnificent people, the hugs, the warmth, the information, the depth of feeling. I remember sensing that something profound was breaking open for me, and I knew I would be somehow different from then on.

When I got home I showered, went to bed, and just started to cry and cry. I cried every time I thought of all the love I had experienced throughout the week, the closeness, the sincere caring, the intimacy, and the high level of emotional awareness. I cried when I realized that the thoughts of me being "rotten at the core," of which I had been so ashamed, were just a result of hurtful conditioning, a cover for all the unshed tears that were now falling freely like a cleansing rain. I was cleaning myself up, freeing myself from all the grief I carried with me all my life, eliminating all the misinformation I had about myself. My body was soaked with sweat, and the tears kept coming as I purged myself of the mistaken belief that I was "no damn good." This was emotional cleansing at work, a re-evaluation of my belief system taking place. I was watching a chronic pattern of mine, with its accompanying set of distress recordings, being dismantled. I had reclaimed the knowledge that I was good, lovable, and worthy of being loved. Sitting there on the bed I felt my brain, like a computer that had been reprogrammed with new information, rapidly scanning every one of my beliefs, getting rid of the old misinformation and replacing it with the new. Every aspect of my life was being re-evaluated, since so many parts were influenced by those negative beliefs. It was exciting, exhilarating, and a little scary. I now had a new point of view about myself. I remember calming down for awhile until my cat and dog, Motors and Bucky, jumped up on the bed together and started licking my face all over. They were the best kind of affirmation and recognition I could have possibly gotten at that moment. The flow of warm tears began once again as I kissed and hugged both of them, realizing how much love the three of us had for each other. I released lots of emotional toxins that day, almost exclusively through tears. I reclaimed a large piece of my humanity and have never lost sight of my goodness since then.

As we go through the adventures of life, we inevitably come face to face with some real losses. Whether we lose a cherished possession, whether we reach the end of a very important friendship, whether we lose the use of a part of our functioning body, or whether we experience the death of a close friend or relative, the intense feelings of loss will trigger—or open the basement door to—all the deep feelings attached to our initial experience of separation. This can be so painful that many of us will do whatever we can to avoid experiencing the pain. But if the emotional toxins are not released, the stored up tension increases even further.

If, on the other hand, we make a decision to face the painful emotions, we will be making a decision that can and probably will benefit us greatly. With support and the basic understanding that the release of emotional toxins is a healing process, we can take the bull by the horns, so to speak, and make another bold move in reclaiming our ability to be in charge of our lives.

Remember, even if you have been numbed out for years, each and every small experience of loss in the present will offer you the opportunity to cleanse your body of deep pools of emotional toxins from the past. This is exactly why so many people get so deeply upset about small and seemingly insignificant things. This is exactly why people go to funerals and cry, even if they never met the person who died. This is why so many people love going to sad movies—because they get to cry about some deep loss from the past.

Although the body will be temporarily relieved of some emotional tension, and almost always feel better after a good cry, my observation is that the healing becomes more permanent and more profound when we understand that a good portion of the tears is indirectly connected to the body's attempt to heal from some old distress or loss.

The feelings need to be felt and the emotional toxins need to be released. Remember, we need no justification to feel a feeling. It is a wonderful—albeit sometimes painful—part of the human experience. Remember also that we can't be sensitive to and feel wonderful, pleasurable emotions without allowing painful emotions to be a part of our full human experience, too. You needn't be held hostage by these emotions anymore. You just need to learn how to handle them.

As an experiment, allow yourself to fully feel an emotion you find painful, without indulging in any dramatic recordings to fit the feeling. For example, if sadness or grief is an emotion you've been avoiding, take a few minutes each day to feel some of the things you're sad about. Most of us carry large amounts of grief from the past that we have unintentionally and unconsciously suppressed. Over the years, the suppressed emotion turns into large pockets of emotional toxins, waiting to be tapped and released. Some feelings of sadness will be sure to bubble up to the surface as you relax into this space. Then, spontaneously, the body will take over and attempt to purge itself of the emotional toxins through the release of tears. This will be easier for some and more difficult for others.

Initially, there will be some awkwardness as you allow yourself to feel some of the grief and sadness you may have been avoiding for so long. But in time, as you practice this, you will develop the ability to release the emotion with little effort and more and more purity, and when pure, it will take a natural course in expression and dissipation.

Obviously, tears need to flow to cleanse our systems, say when a close friend dies. In addition to painful emotions surrounding death, there is deep confusion. Although death is a part of life, I believe most of us are all still deeply confused about why death has to happen at all. The only thing that does make sense here is to allow the feelings of confusion to surface. Too many of us are deeply confused about death, but have no space to feel the confusion. It's OK to not have all the answers. It's OK to admit that sometimes we just don't understand. In effect, if we allow it to, our naivety or ignorance keeps us humble and in awe, on some level, of the wonder, magic, mystery, and adventure of life itself. This is good.

In 1983 my father died. He was eighty-three years old and I think he was ready to go. I had been counseled a great deal on the abuse I had endured at his hands, and had reclaimed a loving, peaceful relationship with him. He had become frail in his later years, and I no longer feared him.

When I heard that he had taken his last breath, instead of crying, which would have felt like a "normal" response, I felt my whole body relax. I felt sad that my father had died, but I was fascinated with my body's response. On some deep level, my body still carried a vast amount of fear. In my cells and muscles and bones, I was still terrified of him. With his death, my body felt incredible relief. That was exactly how I needed to react.

In 1991 my mother died. She died peacefully, in her own bed in her own home in Florida. The last two years of her life were difficult because she didn't want to live anymore. Her death was no surprise, and actually came as a relief. I was totally prepared emotionally and intellectually for her death, or so I thought. When I heard she died, I immediately had an overwhelming surge of grief wash over me like a wave. Before her death, I had been sure that I would have complete control of my emotions, but I was wrong. Untapped pools of tears poured out of me for hours and days. Once again, my body was doing what it needed to do, completely separate from what I thought it needed.

I didn't stop it. In fact, I felt blessed that, in spite of being raised with heavy male conditioning, which methodically numbs out a man to his emotional body, I had done enough work on myself to have reclaimed my body's ability to heal itself. I had freed myself enough to be connected on an emotional level and was able to use my awareness to support my body's healing process. My intelligence had a new sense of respect and humility for this amazing process, gifted to me from birth. I had gotten my misguided control out of my body's way and allowed the healing process to take its natural course.

CHAPTER 2: Trembling

∿∿∿

When I was about eight or nine years old I used to love to go to the beach with my family. I loved playing in the sand and running on the beach. I loved the ocean too, but I was frightened of the water and the power of the waves. Countless times I found myself trembling, with my feet in the shallow water as I watched with excitement and trepidation as one wave after another came crashing in.

"There's nothing to be scared of," my father would blurt out with a patronizing smile on his face. He was trying to be helpful, but he only made me feel worse about myself. His reassurance did not make the trembling stop. I wanted so desperately to show him that I wasn't scared. I felt like I was letting him down somehow by not being able to stop my body from trembling.

Another form of cleansing, trembling (or shaking) is a symptom of the body doing its best to heal from something frightening. Most children are still connected to their body's ability to tremble, but as we grow into adulthood we slowly but surely become anesthetized in this area. We become so detached that most of us don't even remember what it's like to tremble. Those who still have the ability to shake usually do everything possible to hide this body function, feeling shame and embarrassment, quietly believing something is radically wrong with them. In fact, something is right with them. Most people are completely confused about this natural healing function of the body. I have never once met a person who was relaxed and confident about his trembling, with the clear understanding that it was his body's natural way of healing from frightening incidents. From my observations over the years, trembling and shaking are much more unacceptable in our society than crying. In our society crying has a small place, trembling has no place at all.

Going to horror movies and telling scary ghost stories are often unconscious attempts to feel and release some old stored-up fear in a safe environment. Unfortunately, these creative attempts fall short of their intent and, in fact, frequently cause even more damage by leaving another layer of fear and paranoia on top of the old layer.

My friends and I used to love to go to horror movies when we were kids. We'd nervously devour bags of popcorn while quietly doing all we could to suppress our growing anxiety as the tension of the horror movie was building. We were filled with nervous energy, but could not let on. Revealing our terror would have insured us of incredible ridicule from the rest of our group, clearly a fate worse than death at the time. Occasionally there was a movie that scared all of us so badly that we laughed about it for days with no one person being the brunt of our mockery. Most of us would have restless nights for a week or two after an exceptionally scary horror movie. We would have nightmares that would leave us exhausted, and day fantasies that would often continue the terrified feelings. We couldn't talk about it much, though, and thus we never got the chance to heal from the upset to our systems.

Being numb and looking good, rather than being seen as scared, was much more appealing to us. Although we did our best to look calm and in control on the surface, we usually had horrible nightmares as the terror oozed out while we were sleeping and were less in control.

In all my years of counseling I have never met an individual who was not afraid of something, whether he knew it or not.

Years ago, working at a crisis intervention center, during a quiet period my shift partner and I began to discuss fear. Dimitri was a strong, lean, muscular man of thirty-five, who had travelled the planet and had some quite fascinating adventures. I was trying my best to explain to him that every human being has some things that he or she is scared of; that fear is simply part of the emotional body that all human beings were born with.

He refused to accept any piece of my point of view, using well-thought-out logic to confidently and quite arrogantly invalidate my thoughts. "Marty," he then said with a patronizing smile, "when you've climbed the highest mountains in the world and you've come within inches of your death, you just don't have fears that run your life anymore." I felt a little frustrated and took a break from the conversation. Ten minutes later, as irony would have it, a woman whom Dimitri was very interested in dating walked into the crisis center. He froze and just sat there speechless.

If you're willing to admit, at least to yourself and a few close friends, that you get scared, then you have a chance of freeing yourself from the grips of fear. If you want to experiment with releasing some fear in a healthy and playful way, go to an amusement park with a few of your buddies. I've done this occasionally and it works pretty well most of the time. It's not a cure-all, but it will give you a picture, a little window to notice that it is possible to release fear.

Most amusement parks have some kind of House of Horrors. They're supposed to be really scary, right? Go through the House of Horrors, but agree ahead of time with your buddies to stay very close to each other, even holding hands if you feel all right about that. Then when you get to parts of the house that are scary, scream out loud together. Keep screaming until you start laughing and shaking. It probably won't take too long. Keep going through the horror house while in touch with your buddies, and scream loudly and as much as you want to whenever something scary comes floating your way. If I'm right, you'll sweat and laugh and shake a bunch, and when you come out of the house you'll proba-bly feel exhilarated.

Over sixty years ago, President Roosevelt said in a speech to the people of the United States, "We have nothing to fear but fear itself." Fear that is not released turns into powerlessness. We often tend to rationalize our strange behavior rather than take an honest look at the things that we fear. Suppressed fear is a silent destroyer of lives.

If you make the decision to not allow fear to rule your life, then you must also make the choice to be open to your body's natural healing process—trembling.

- The first step in unravelling the confusion and inhibitions you have in this area is to admit that you have fears. Common euphemisms used to distract ourselves from the fear that we are actually feeling are "nervous," "anxious," "very concerned," "worried," etc. Admit that you're afraid of something. It doesn't matter what you are scared of, although being frightened of benign things like mice, bugs, or the dark, are initially easier to work with than ominous issues like nuclear war, AIDS, death, or rape.

- Find a friend to exchange stories with and then tell each other about all the things that you are scared of. When we tell another person about our fears, it usually allows us to feel them a little more. It also opposes the irrational behavior of hiding our fears. Initially we might feel some embarrassment or shame when we reveal our fears to a friend. The key here is that your friend should listen to you with no judgment at all. He or she needs to maintain an attitude of relaxed acceptance. Then you will have safety to continue.

- You may begin to tremble at this point. This is good. Your job now is to acknowledge to yourself, in spite of the usual discomfort, that this is good. The trembling is actually an indication that emotional toxins are being released. As you continue the trembling you may have old memories come up. Those are important memories, probably associated in some way with the release of emotional toxins. Write them down and talk about them. They've popped up to assist you in your emotional cleansing. Treat the memories as gifts to accelerate your healing.

- For those of you who are not able to tremble easily, you need to be a little creative. Your ability to tremble is in tact. It may just need a bit of a jump start. Making sounds as if you were really scared tends to work rather well. Different sounds will work for different people. There's no formula here. My observation is that each person knows what sounds to make that will bring on the trembling.

- Notice any rigidity in your body. Your shoulders might be up to your ears, you might have your eyes closed, your neck might be tensed, your back might be bent over. This is all a result of being scared but not allowing your body to shake. Your job here is to notice where you're tight and slowly loosen whatever areas are constricted. This will free up your body to tremble and allow the emotional toxins to be released even more. Check on your breathing, too. Many people stop breathing when they feel some fear. This is a very good place to encourage a friend or friends to help you. Often they will notice your tension before you do.

- When you decide to end the releasing session take a few minutes to notice colors or objects in the room. Run your hands along the rug or the floor and notice the texture, hug someone, have a bite to eat, or do something else comforting. The idea here is to focus your attention away from what you were just trembling about and on something that will help ground you. Remember, you've carried stored-up tension for years and you will not free your body of it in one session. The process will take time. There's really no rush. If you slowly and methodically integrate the cleansing process into your life, you will have redirected your body and mind toward health and well-being.

- Appreciate yourself for taking the risk of facing some fears. It takes courage to do this work, and you deserve to compliment yourself.

- If appropriate, make sure your friend gets the same amount of time in her turn, and make a decision to be completely present for her. In many situations we learn as much from listening to a friend as we do from our own processing.

- Check in with yourself a few times each day. Take a minute to notice what kind of thoughts are going on inside your head. Ask yourself if any thoughts are filled with anxiety or worry. These are fear thoughts. If you can identify and label any fear thoughts, irrational worries, or anxieties, then you can also tell yourself that they have no positive value for you. This process will help you methodically weed out the thoughts that don't serve you well.

In time, you'll reclaim your ability to tremble, and you'll also adjust your belief system so that you can be relaxed and accepting of your body's healing process. You'll notice more and more frightening things that go on in your life, however you'll now have the ability to keep functioning thoughtfully. You can get scared, tremble, but continue to go after all the things that make your life worth living.

CHAPTER 3: Raging

Raging, with short, loud outbursts and often a thin layer of sweat over the body, is an indication of the releasing of emotional tension from the experience of some form of powerlessness or deep frustration. Raging is a harmless and innocent form of releasing emotional tension and is a form of healing. Unfortunately, it is often confused with acts of aggression that are destructive to property or people. Destructive acts are irrational and have no redeeming healing value. The key to releasing our rage is learning to get the emotional toxins out without hurting anyone, including ourselves.

Years ago, when I was losing my sight, I went bowling with some friends. My vision was pretty bad that day and I bowled an eighty-two. I was so filled with frustration and fury, but managed to hold it in all the way home. I was burning inside, though, just waiting for an opportunity to explode. When we got home I threw the door open, ran into my bedroom, grabbed one of my bowling trophies and was going to smash it against the wall in a dramatic expression of my frustration. But instead, the hand of the trophy punctured my skin when I grabbed it. I was bleeding pretty badly, went to the hospital, and received four stitches to close up the wound.

We've had so many poor models in the area of releasing anger. We've been trained to either blame ourselves for things that have gone wrong, or to blame others. When we blame ourselves, the anger is internalized and we usually hurt ourselves in some way. When we blame others, we tend to dramatize our frustration at someone and often do something that hurts them. Both attempts to free ourselves of the painful emotions are misdirected. The key is to find a way to express the feelings along with releasing the emotional toxins, without hurting others or ourselves.

Lots of people allow frustration to rule their lives, raging out of control and hurting friends and family. This inappropriate and often unaware attempt to free themselves of the toxins they carry only causes more negativity and commonly leads to illness and disease. Others feel anger, but are too scared to express it in healthy ways to others. Instead of getting it out, they tend to focus the anger inward. This inward rage very often depletes the immune system and,very much like the externally focused raging, may cause harm, frequently resulting in a pattern of psycho-somatic illnesses.

I knew of two highly regarded doctors, one from Hawaii, the other from Florida, who were both successful in their bouts with cancer. They both were confident in their belief in what healed them. They both felt strongly that it had to do with their understanding of anger and expression of rage.

The doctor from Hawaii was sure that inhibiting his anger, cutting it off as soon as he could, was the key to reclaiming his health. The doctor from Florida was convinced that he reclaimed his good health because he learned to let his anger out the moment he felt it.

The two stories are not in conflict with each other. I believe both doctors were correct. The physical healing took place in both doctors because they figured out how to be responsible with the rage in their lives. I think the doctor from Hawaii was contradicting early conditioning that compelled him to make messes with frequent dramatic outbursts of rage. This out-of-control, irrational exploding was causing his body to be out of control with toxins, emotional and physical, which may very well have led to the cancer, directly or indirectly.

The doctor from Florida was conditioned to hold everything in, especially his rage. It's quite possible that his early training to constantly suppress rage eventually caused an imbalance in his body, which, once again, directly or indirectly might very well have led to his cancer.

Releasing rage in healthy ways is crucial to us. It can have deep connections to living powerful lives, expressing our sexuality fully, experiencing healthy intensity and sharp focus. It certainly will help us think more flexibly and relate more rationally with others.

If you are the type that is repulsed by anger and have gotten into a pattern of denial and pretense about your rage:

- Ask yourself questions like, "What's been pissing me off lately?" and "What can't I stand about ...?" Also, "What am I sick and tired of?" These questions will get you to notice where your frustrations lie in the present.
- Tell yourself that you're angry or frustrated about those things. This will help you get in touch with the emotion of anger. Remember, the feeling of anger is all right. It's the destructive drama scenes that are not acceptable. Admit that you're angry. This will help combat denial and destroy pretense.
- Call a friend and tell him or her that you are angry. This will

break down the pretense even more, contradicting the habit of hiding this from others. Make sure your friend will listen without judging you for having the feeling. It's probably a good idea to get a prior agreement about doing this with that friend. It's also important that he or she promise to listen to you about your anger for a short period of time—probably five or ten minutes, not much more at first. Exchanging listening time is always a good idea. You get to build safety with each other and nobody gets burnt out from listening all the time. This is an excellent beginning, especially if you can respect each other's need for confidentiality, and you promise to never discuss the issues that the other person worked on unless your friend brings them up first. This will help develop mutual respect and trust.

- If you decide that you'd like to release emotional toxins on a deeper level, cleansing your system of stored-up toxins held in for years, I encourage you to find a good counselor or someone who has done prior work on releasing rage. It's important to work with a trusted guide, which is what a good counselor really is. Whether you decide to stomp your feet, yell, hit pillows, kick balls, or wrestle with your friend, you probably will begin to get very warm. You might have loud outbursts along with some trembling, some tears, or even some laughter. This is the releasing of emotional toxins taking place. Any activity that causes physical pain for you or your friend in any way during the process is not going to provide the safety needed for the toxins to release purely. It's important that both people are sensitive to this.

- After some releasing, stop and get in touch with your body. How do you feel? How is your breathing? What do you physically need at this moment?

- Check in with your friend. Ask him or her to tell you a few things they like about you. This will give you important information about how your friend is doing. You'll find out if he or she is still present with you and you'll get to hear some compliments in addition. This is helpful because we often feel bad about ourselves when we let this toxic stuff out. Those bad feelings are not who we really are, but they are fragments of old accumulated toxins, bringing up just how bad we were made to feel about ourselves.

- End this period of work with being nice to yourself. Take the time to focus your attention on lightness, whatever that means to you. This will balance out the heavy feeling that may persist from the prior work. I often have clients look around the room, describing different colors and objects. Move around, get a drink, have something to eat, get some fresh air. I encourage you to wait until all your attention is back. You'll know it. Then appreciate your effort, your courage for doing the work, and appreciate your friend.

If you're someone who frequently feels angry, occasionally exploding, losing your temper and hurting people you care about:

- Admit to yourself that you have lots of anger, but that you also have choices about what to do with that emotion. You do not need to feel bad about yourself for having anger. Usually bad feelings about yourself will falsely seem justified when you express your anger in ways that hurt other people or yourself.

- When you're feeling angry, notice what goes on in your body: your breathing, your blood flow, your muscle constriction, your body posture. The feeling of anger sets off physiological reactions, many that are depleting to the immune system, especially if experienced on a regular basis.

- Challenge yourself to develop the ability to slow those body reactions down with slow breathing, visualization, meditation, or any method of your own liking. This will help you realize that you can have control over your own body. This is the beginning of developing real power.

- Find a friend or two who will listen to you on the phone or in person whenever you feel angry. Often five or ten minutes of blowing off steam will be all that's needed to shift the energy. Get a prior agreement so that you don't have to explain anything when you're feeling anger. Our best attempts at communicating don't work very well when we're filled with intense emotion. Phrases like "I'm feeling angry. Can you listen for a few minutes?" work best.

- If you choose to pursue the release of long-held emotional toxins, I encourage you to get involved with a support group or a private counselor. A good support group will help you see that you're not alone with this struggle. It's also a powerful learning experience to watch others grow in this area. A private counselor who has done work on releasing rage in healthy ways can also be useful.

- Appreciate yourself frequently for having the courage to face this difficult and painful part of your old conditioning. Then learn to be thoughtful and nurturing to yourself in lots of different ways. This is an important step.

CHAPTER 4: Laughter

Laughter, the most acceptable of the healing processes, often is an indication of the releasing of emotional tension from an experience of embarrassment, ridicule, shame, or humiliation. Laughter is always a function that releases tension in the body, and it also occurs when people are happy and playing or simply having fun.

One of the best tributes to the healing power of laughter is the autobiographical book by Norman Cousins, *Anatomy of an Illness.* Throughout the book, Cousins talks about how he used laughter everyday to help him heal from a serious illness.

I know of a California therapist who invested lots of time learning about the subtleties of laughter and its healing effect on the body. She used to go around the country leading workshops on laughter, helping people break through their inhibitions and confusion regarding this powerful healing process.

Belly laughs are the key here. Most of us have been so ridiculed for showing any intense emotion that we've even inhibited our laughter. When we are free to release tension through laughing, our bodies often respond with quivering in the belly and tears rolling down our faces.

Laughter was the only form of healing that I was not forced to inhibit as a child. Through the distress-filled years at home growing up in Brooklyn, I used laughter unawarely to help my body release tension.

I remember eating dinner at my house when I was between the ages of nine and fourteen. My parents would be wiped out from a long day at work and had very little attention for my older sister, Mattie, or me. We managed to find ways to amuse ourselves, however. We'd try to make each other laugh by doing subtle things that weren't obvious but nevertheless would send one of us into an uncontrollable bout of laughter.

One scene got played out over and over again during those years. We used to always have milk at dinner, and my sister had an uncanny knack of making me laugh while I was in the process of drinking. I'd be halfway through a guzzle when I'd glance over at her. Through the corner of my eye I'd see her with a devilish grin on her face, her eyes aglow, staring right at me. That would always crack me up. Milk would come streaming out my nose and onto my plate and the table. My father would leap up and start yelling at me, but his yelling never inhibited my laughter. In this case, he seemed to have no power over me. I'd fall off the chair and be rolling on the floor out of control, with tears gushing down my face. He'd continue to yell, ordering me into my room. I'd get up and wander back to my room, missing the rest of the meal, but never regretting the outburst. I always felt a little lighter, and life appeared a little more enjoyable after those scenes.

Forced laughter is not healing. Invalidating, oppressive jokes are a weak and misdirected attempt to bring laughter and lightness to a group. Most of the time it doesn't work. When you've reclaimed your ability to have deep belly laughs from innocent situations, you won't feel the need to participate in oppressive jokes and degrading laughter. It just won't feel right.

Many jokes are innocent and enjoyable, but these, too, hardly ever get us to the real belly laughs that are healing to the body. The healing process resulting from laughter is most effective when warm tears stream down our faces and our bellies gyrate out of control.

Frequently in the course of recovering all our healing processes we come up against a layer of embarrassment. This will commonly inhibit our body's ability to release. In this society we have been conditioned to be embarrassed about our natural body functions— tears, trembling, and raging, as well as yawning, sweating, burping, and farting. We have wonderful bodies that do amazing things to maintain health and well-being. We need to embrace our bodies with a new, healthier attitude, being fascinated with and appreciative of their uniqueness and complexities.

If you feel embarrassed about any of your body functions:

- Notice that almost all the other bodies on the planet do the same things that your body does. This will help you realize that you are not alone.
- Notice how your body feels when you hold in a burp, a fart, urine, or a bowel movement. Holding things in usually hurts the body, impeding its healthy cleansing of toxins. It's tiring as well because you need to constrict muscles to sustain the forced holding. After awhile, release whatever you've been holding. Most bodies feel relieved when they get to release. This is the body doing what comes naturally. The muscles relax and the toxins are released. It's not too complicated.
- Find a friend or two who will listen to you with no judgment

while you talk about your body functions. Ideally, you will find friends who will be willing to be listened to about their body functions as well. The exchange of listening time develops safety quickly and effectively. It's usually harder to discuss and examine your body functions with others because of our conditioning. This is where the embarrassment usually pops up. If you can talk about this with a friend, your body sensing the safety, you most likely will start giggling about it. Here's where the laughter as a healing process begins to do its job. The more you and your friend laugh about this, the more you and your friend will become relaxed about your body functions, especially with each other.

• Memories or phrases may appear in your mind. These often will be clues to the trail back to where you initially got hurt or misinformed about your body. Follow the trail by talking about the memories or phrases. They inevitably will lead you to other memories. Now that you've broken down the inhibiting wall of embarrassment, it's possible that tears, trembling, or other emotions will spontaneously arise. Your body has gotten the message that you are ready to release. With this new information, the long held emotional toxins will begin to surface, just like the body sweating out physical toxins.

• Remember to be easy with yourself as you reclaim your body's natural healing ability. The tendency may be to rush in and clean up as much as you can as fast as you can. Imagine someone who gets turned on to running. If he immediately attempts to run a marathon he will overwhelm his body and cause damage. His enthusiasm for the sport could diminish quickly if he pulls a muscle or is sore for a week. The same is true in the emotional realm. You need to slowly but methodically develop your emotional muscles before you can thoughtfully run a marathon.

Laughter is probably the most enjoyable of the healing process-es, and is not any less important than the others. Once you reclaim your ability to have deep belly laughs with tears running down your face, you will be on the path toward a lighter, more playful lifestyle.

CHAPTER 5: Touch
∾∾∾

We all have inherent in us the need to touch and to be touched. Our closest ancestors, the apes, chimpanzees, and monkeys, are always seen in groups, grooming each other. We have the same need, but once again our society encourages isolation and separation, rather than supporting the natural way for us to be with each other. Massage therapists will tell you how starved for touch most of their clients are. People who go for massages have recognized their deep need for touch, and are wise enough to be getting this need met.

A large majority of our population is not aware of the health benefits of touch. The body carries more tension and actually takes on a numbness or a board-like stiffness with a lack of touch. When I hug someone, I can tell in a minute if the person has been receiving a healthy amount of touch in his or her life. Most of us are really starving for this basic need to be met, but often we feel bad about ourselves for wanting to touch others and to be touched. This is a good example of how confusing our conditioning has been.

I have many friends who are blind. A majority of them are independent, holding down decent jobs and participating in communi-ty activities with friends and families. Most of them get around on their own fairly well with either a guide dog or a cane. However, I am often saddened and frustrated when I hug them because I can feel how stiff their bodies are and how uncomfortable some of them are with touch. Some of their bodies are wound so tight from the normal daily tension, along with the added stress of getting around without sight. It's not too different for sighted people who live up-tempo, high-stress lives—and most of them, sighted or blind, are not aware of the amount of tension their bodies are carrying. Sometimes we know what we need, but feel very timid and don't know how to break through our own isolation. Sometimes we are just unaware of this need that our body has. Wouldn't it be great if we all could incorporate more safe hugging and touching in our lives?

Over the last few years, some hospitals and private practice doctors have been hiring more and more massage therapists to assist patients in their healing. Studies keep proving, over and over again, the positive healing effects from massage and thoughtful touch, yet its recognition is still not widely accepted. This simple, pure need for touch is also cost-effective. A good part of medical care is based on drugs and surgery, which can be expensive, yet we've found that massage and aware touch often reduce the need for those more costly forms of intervention.

A couple of years ago, when I was single and living alone, I had a series of disturbing sex dreams, one after the other, during a two-week period. The dreams were filled with exciting erotica, romance, and great feelings. I'd wake up, day after day, feeling a little embar-rassed about having unconsciously used some of my dearest female friends as my fantasy lovers. But, "what the hell," I had thought. "No harm done..."

After doing my best to remember every little detail of each dream, I would get up and begin the day, only to be overwhelmed with loneliness. Whenever a friend came over, the loneliness would temporarily disappear, but would return almost immediately after my friend would leave. I'd be back alone and thrust right into the pain of unwanted isolation. This happened time and time again with different friends. When they were hanging out with me, everything was fine, and when they left, the lonely feelings would come right back.

I had enough awareness to observe my thoughts and feelings during this period and noticed how good it felt, when I was with my friends, to receive their attention and to give my attention back to them. We'd listen to each other while eating or going for a walk, discussing the latest interests in our lives. I surmised the good feelings were due to the implied message that we were giving each other—probably something like "I'm glad you're alive and I'm glad you're in my life."

One day I noticed that my loneliness stayed away for a long time after a visit by one of my friends. I was relaxed, at peace with myself, and functioning very well with no sign of the lonely feelings. I slowed down and thought about the few hours that we had spent together. What was different? What had happened to get me to feel so relaxed and so good about myself?

After a couple of minutes of thought, I remembered that we had massaged each other. There was nothing sexual about our exchange, just two good friends giving and receiving some thoughtful touch. She had gone to school to learn about massage and was practicing her new skills on me. Although I had very little knowledge about massage at the time, I did my best to return the favor.

I got excited when I realized that it was the touch my body had received that made the difference. My whole being was calmer because I had been touched by someone in a caring, thoughtful way. All that time previous to our massage exchange, my body was starving to be touched and I never had a clue.

During the next week, I set up "aware touch" exchanges with some of my friends and, sure enough, got the same results. Sometimes we exchanged hand massages for ten minutes or so. Other times we exchanged foot massages, back massages, head rubs, some cuddling while watching TV, etc. The results were consistent and profound. Not only was my body much more relaxed than before, with my mind functioning more clearly, but the lonely feelings had been greatly diminished and I completely stopped having those confusing sex dreams. I still was single and wished I were in a relationship, but I wasn't haunted by the loneliness that so many single people struggle with. Also, I understood that what I thought to be my obsessive desire for sex turned out to be a simple need to be touched on a regular basis.

In the next month, I made a decision to go to massage school, and then completed an excellent five-month course at the Florida School of Massage in Gainesville. I received more massages during that five-month period than I had in my whole life. My body loved every minute of it! I also learned to be a pretty good massage therapist in the process.

Toward the end of the course we got a chance to do massage on people we didn't know. Once a week, residents of the city were invited, for a small fee, to experience an hour massage from the students.

One day I got to work on a man, about sixty-five years old. He was very tense throughout his body, but was able to relax and enjoy the massage. Most of his body just needed some oil, some soft, thoughtful touching, and some manipulation of his muscles and the soft tissue before relaxing and bouncing back to a healthier state. However, his feet fascinated me. His feet carried lots of tension that caused his toes to point in the direction of his head. I worked on his feet and legs quite a bit, but was not able to get those muscles to loosen up. He had fallen asleep toward the last half of the massage, but the muscles still refused to relax. It was amazing to me to think that he could be sleeping, totally unconscious and out of aware control, but the muscles stayed locked up, frozen in a state of contraction.

I'm sure that he could have loosened those muscles up in time with regular massage, good nutrition, and an exercise regimen. The fascinating thing to me was that his muscles were locked in a contracted position whether he was awake or asleep. That's what can happen to our bodies if we don't take care of them.

I now have touch in my life on a regular basis, giving and receiving it in a caring way with most of my friends.

I don't know that much about the physiology of what takes place when one person touches another, but the results are clear. When there is skin-to-skin contact, and it happens in a thoughtful, caring way, we experience healing energy on many levels. Our bodies relax more, the daily tension drains away. Our heart rate slows down and becomes more regular. When we experience safe touch, it seems to be soothing to our whole being. We feel cared for in a very special way. Exchanging this kind of aware touching through massage is a wonderful way to develop more intimacy in all your relationships. The beginning words in the rock opera "Tommy" say it all in a nutshell. "See me. Feel me. Touch me. Heal me."

CHAPTER 6: Help

For years I led workshops for blind, visually impaired people, and allies. (What I mean by "allies" here are people with no visual impairment who have decided to make friends with, learn from, be of assistance to, and support blind and visually impaired people.) I designed these workshops to help break down the barriers between the two groups. In the early going at one of the workshops, I immediately observed a growing tension stirred up when the visually impaired people needed to ask the group of allies for help to get around the workshop site. It seemed logical that, since the visually impaired consistently had to ask for help, they might have some distressed thoughts and feelings in this area. So I asked a few blind people to talk about what they liked and what they couldn't stand about asking for help.

They complained about feeling like a burden, not believing anybody really wanted to help them, feeling ugly and repulsive, and assuming the people who were assisting them were concerned about the clinginess and neediness of the blind. I figured this response, but did not expect the reaction of the abled-bodied allies.

Lots of them were filled with emotions when hearing the struggles of the blind people. There was electricity going on in the room, so I decided to call up a few more folks.

I asked a few allies to talk about what got jiggled for them. Amazingly, each one of them identified completely with the struggles of the blind. They, too, complained of never feeling okay about asking for help, of feeling nobody had the time to help them, of believing that nobody would care enough when they really needed help. They also said they had the added burden of needing to appear like they had it all together because there was nothing physically wrong with them. They actually appeared to be a little envious of the visually impaired group. They said they felt most people, in general, were much more understanding toward the needs of the blind and were much more willing to be of help to anyone with a disability.

After that workshop, I formulated a small paragraph to help contradict the powerful pull to comply with society's rigidities around asking for help.

"I promise to always ask for help whenever I need it, and to receive the help graciously whenever it's offered. When help is needed but not forthcoming, I will persist in asking others until I receive the help I need. If, by chance, help is offered to me but not required, I will firmly, but lovingly, refuse the assistance offered."

Ever since, I have begun my workshops by revealing to everyone the difficulties that arise when any of us needs help. I'll usually work with one or two people, beginning with having them talk about any distressed thoughts or feelings they have around asking for and receiving help. Occasionally, I'll direct them toward looking at any early memories as a child that could have confused or distorted their views regarding this. I always strongly encourage those in attendance at the workshop to act, for the weekend, on the content in the "help" paragraph.

The results have been consistently uplifting. For a whole weekend, people get to experience an environment with everybody asking for help and doing their best to receive it graciously. I encourage those who usually give help to make it a point to ask for help at least a few times during the workshop. They initially tend to feel quite awkward about this, but usually get more relaxed with it as the weekend unfolds.

In general, this is an excellent technique to begin to break down the thick walls of isolation. I've discovered one perplexing obstacle, however. The first part of the paragraph begins with the words "I promise to always ask for help whenever I need it..." Some people are so disconnected, due to their earlier conditioning, that they often don't know when they really need help.

Years ago, a few friends and I were sitting at a table overlooking a few tennis courts. It started pouring and four of us began to huddle under a small overhang above the table. One friend just stood there in the rain, getting totally soaked from head to toe. When we encouraged him to get under the overhang with us, he responded casually by saying "Nah, I'm all right." He just stood there getting soaked. I watched in disbelief while big raindrops bounced off his head. The next day he came down with a bad cold.

We can analyze strange behavior like that until we're blue in the face. I don't think that would be useful here. What is significant is to understand that we all have disconnected places where we don't realize that we could use some help. If we just make the decision to notice a few places where help would make things go better, we will be redirecting our attention toward health and well-being. As you focus more on noticing where you could use some help, your sensitivity in this area will slowly begin to grow—away from an isolated life and toward human connection.

I've heard a delightful as well as captivating description of the difference between heaven and hell. At a long banquet table with people sitting on both sides, there are huge amounts of incredible delicacies, but everybody at the table is starving. They have long-handled utensils and can't manage to get the food into their mouths. That's hell.

Heaven is the same scene, but the people sitting at the banquet table are all smiling, relaxed and fully satisfied. They learned the lesson of "help" by feeding each other from across the table.

The banquet-table story is well known, yet most people who have heard it are still compelled to do too many things on their own. So many of us are reluctant to ask for help, fearing rejection or negative judgment. Maybe because of negative childhood fables. One of the most confusing stories I heard growing up was about the boy who cried "wolf."

I think this story left many children confused about when to ask for help. How bad do things have to get before asking for help will be seen as a reasonable request? I think the attitude for years in our society has been "don't ask for help unless you really need it." This has inhibited us all with regard to asking for assistance and support.

Instead of spending a long time analyzing the historical significance of this attitude, I encourage you to break out of the restrictive box and start asking for any kind of help that will make your life better. Remember, when you ask someone for help you give that person a chance to make a difference in your life. Learning to give and receive help among friends will also assist you in developing deeper friendships. It may be awkward at first, and you may not always receive the help that you ask for, but I promise that the results down the road will be fruitful. Healthy relationships must have places where both people can feel safe to show each other their vulnerabilities. Asking for help makes people feel vulnerable. This is not a bad thing. On the contrary, this is a very good thing. The only reason this "help" piece is hard is because of old distresses and confusing misinformation from the past.

No relationship can reach an honest, equal, intimate connection if one of the partners stays closed and refuses to take the risk of showing vulnerability. The development of safe, trusting relationships is a crucial ingredient in continuing effective emotional cleansing work.

One day I went into a bathroom and was startled by the sound of a fly buzzing by the window. It was frantically trying to get out of the bathroom, but kept bumping into the screen. That was the obstacle in the way of freedom for the imprisoned fly. I watched for what seemed to be about ten long minutes while the fly attempted in vain, over and over again, to break through the barrier to freedom. The fly could obviously see and smell the vast outdoors, clearly where it belonged, but could not figure out how to get there.

Right next to the window with the screen was another window, also open, but with no screen at all. It was less than a foot away, but for the fly, who couldn't see past its own little narrow view of the world, the window might as well have not been there.

I watched, fascinated by the scene, until I reached down, caught the fly, and moved my hand a foot to the right. I opened my hand in front of the window with no screen, and the fly lifted off and buzzed forward, just like it did so many times before. It flew out the open window toward freedom and was gone in a flash.

I thought some about that fly. It was doing its very best to live, but found itself hopelessly trapped in the bathroom, on the inside of the window. Freedom and "the good life" were right past that screen, but the fly couldn't figure out how to get there on its own.

Maybe the fly would have eventually, haphazardly, stumbled its way to the open window and out, maybe not. But this fly was lucky. There was someone around who had a bigger, more aware picture of the whole scene and was also willing to help the fly to freedom.

Some of my most joyful moments as a counselor occur when I'm being aware enough and competent enough to assist someone toward freedom. People are not as simple as flies, though. I had to catch the fly before I could assist him toward freedom. He was totally vulnerable, with his life literally in my hand. Very often, people won't trust a counselor enough to allow him or her to help. For lots of people, it's just too scary to be that vulnerable. Other times, counselors will help free their clients from the distresses that have been making their lives miserable, only to find that the person has chosen to go back to the imprisoned, distress-riddled situation. I find these situations incredibly frustrating.

One of my teachers told me, "I'll do whatever I can to help those who are sleeping in the cave. I'll wake them up and slowly walk them out of the darkness and into the light. I'll stay with them awhile until they can fend for themselves with their newly found strength and awareness. But, if they choose to go back into the cave, I will not go after them again." Take the risk. Reach out. Ask for help.

CHAPTER 7: Subtle Hidden Cleansers

Space and Time

When we interrupt our own destructive behavior, we often come face to face with a void—a space where we are not acting in the old, patterned way, but where we haven't yet figured out what kind of actions or behavior to replace the old, patterned behavior with. Here it's crucial to stay with the "nothingness." If we can make friends with the void, we will be more empowered to refuse any pull to repeat the old, negative behavior. We will then be able to make a smart decision about how we want to fill the space.

I have counseled many people who have done good work toward permanently transforming their lives. I've watched some of them valiantly break through the old destructive behavior and go on to flourish, living lives filled with joy. Others have made similar breakthroughs, only to retreat back into the old destructive lifestyle. I think the difference had to do with the way they handled this space of nothingness.

Why do many of us have such a difficult time with this void, this period of time when we've given up something that we really didn't want, but have not yet replaced it with what we do want? Because the unknown is scary to most of us. We've had too many past experiences where it led to some form of pain. Uncertainty is also where the magic of life is, but it's hard for many of us to trust that the void of not knowing will lead us to joyful surprises.

I remember going through one of those periods of transition in my life. I had been working at a crisis intervention center for eight years. The staff had gone through many uncomfortable changes and the organization was leaning toward getting involved in things I didn't believe in. So I resigned. I didn't know what I was going to do, but I felt good about leaving. I believed that I was cleansing my life of what had become a toxic situation for me, but the large space in my life that had been filled with the crisis work was now open, with nothing to immediately replace it.

A couple of weeks went by and I found myself slowly losing my center, my balance. I was no longer so confident that my decision to resign was such a good idea. Doubt had begun to slowly seep into my mind. I didn't know if I should aggressively seek some other work to fill my days or if I should just relax and trust that things would naturally evolve. I chose to relax and trust, still somewhat confident that this was the right decision, but after a few more weeks of nothingness I began to doubt my latest decision as well. I couldn't tell if I was procrastinating about doing something new. When I thought of moving, it felt like compulsively rushing. When I thought about relaxing and trusting, it felt like procrastination. I was between a rock and a hard place.

Things eventually shifted for me, as things do. Shift usually happens, although when you're going through that transition period it often feels like you'll be there for an eternity. This is where the concept of time comes into play.

When I was in college many years ago, I used to tell people that I was taking up time and space, my way of saying that I was goofing off in school and had no real direction. Looking back, I wish that I had been able to take a course all about time and space. I don't think it's fair to talk about space without discussing time and its effect on us as well.

When we're totally engaged in joyful activities, time seems to fly by. When we're in excruciating pain, ten minutes seems like an eternity. The passing of time—seconds, minutes, hours, days—is an agreed-to standard around the world. But how we, as individuals, perceive time varies greatly. Our perception of it is influenced by numerous things, including feelings, thoughts, behavior, physical sensations, and past experiences.

Some of us feel as if we're going through a period of transition quickly, while others will feel like they're going extremely slowly. Each person needs to stay cognizant of his or her body rhythms and perceptions of fast and slow as transition is dealt with. The void of nothingness and the time it takes us to shift from destructive behavior to healthier behavior are really not the problem. The real problem seems to be how we handle ourselves while going through space and time. Do we drive ourselves crazy with self-criticism and nervous anxiety, or can we find ways to be thoughtful and nurturing to ourselves while in the process of transition?

Peacefully cleansing a space: Many people use sage to cleanse a room or a house. It is a ritual aimed at detoxifying a space from old, possibly negative energy. I do not know if there are actually physical benefits from burning sage, but it seems to be quite healing for people, emotionally and spiritually. It's important to find some way, whether in the form of ritual or not, to find peace with space when in transition.

Peacefully taking our time: Many cultures have a fixed period of time to mourn the loss of a loved one. Eight days is standard in the Jewish tradition. Whatever the transition, each situation calls for a peaceful understanding and acceptance of the time that you'll need to complete the healing. We often need to grieve for weeks and months when we lose a loved one. Judgments are mind games and a waste of time. If the body needs to take more time to purge, to cleanse emotionally, then that's what it needs to do.

It's difficult to sustain our own natural body rhythm in this fast-paced society. We are compelled to go faster, to rush. The only time rushing makes sense to me is when I'm in the middle of the street and a truck's barrelling down the road in my direction.

Attention

Time and space are abstract concepts that we need to think about before our minds are able to make good use of them. Another abstract but important concept we need to understand is how the use of attention can help or hurt our lives.

In the seventies, I had a good friend who was diagnosed with inoperable stomach cancer. Darcy was deeply involved in counseling, with many experienced counselors as friends. The news about her terminal cancer was obviously devastating to her. Darcy told me, however, that she never believed she would actually die from the disease.

She took two months off from her work to focus on healing her body from the cancer. She went on a strict diet and counseled for a number of hours on her condition every day. She asked her husband, Peter, to screen all the people who had wanted to offer her counseling time. Darcy was sure she could heal, but wanted to do her best to set up a healthy environment for her planned recovery.

Peter methodically screened over thirty people who wanted to be supportive to Darcy. The most important question he asked them was, "Do you believe that Darcy will be able to be cured of cancer?" Only those who truly believed that Darcy would heal completely were allowed to spend time with her.

Darcy used the impeccable attention from her friends for eight weeks as she grieved deeply, trembled profusely, raged, and laughed on occasion about her life-threatening situation. After the two months, she went back to the doctor for a check-up. The doctor was stunned and fascinated that the stomach cancer had completely disappeared. Her body had healed with no sign left of the dreaded disease.

Darcy told me later she was sure the wonderful attention of her friends and counselors, and their total confidence in her ability to heal, made the difference for her. Twenty years later she is doing fine, living well in Europe.

Relaxed attention has incredible power. Your ability to heal is enhanced greatly when you receive relaxed attention from another human being who believes in you and your ability to heal. The opposite is true also.

The power of Voodoo has to do with the power of attention—negative attention. A curse is more effective when the person who has been cursed knows about it. His fears turn into negative attention focused inward. The curse is even more potent when the whole town knows about it. The cursed person receives a continuous barrage of negative attention wherever he goes, from the innocent townspeople who fear for his life. This is incredibly debilitating, weakening the immune system of the cursed, and often insuring that the curse comes true.

When I worked at the crisis intervention center in Woodstock, occasionally five to ten staff members would be hanging out in the back room, passing the time. The social scene was quite enjoyable for me, except when I needed to go to the bathroom.

I was the only blind person there, and whenever I got up to move, all conversation would stop. Everybody would be staring at my body as I moved to go around the corner to the bathroom. I knew my way around the building just fine, but when everybody stared, I'd get shaky. I distinctly recall feeling weighed down and dizzy a few times from the combination of the group's concerned attention for me and my personal reaction to their stares. They were good people, innocently worrying about the blind man's well-being. To me, however, the effects were quite intense.

In Edgar Cayce's prophetic readings, he stated repeatedly that the mind was builder as well as destroyer. I believe the aspect of the mind that he was referring to is its ability to focus attention. The mind has the ability to build when it focuses its attention on positive things, to destroy when it focuses on the negative. Our lives are greatly influenced by the choice of what we focus our powerful attention on.

Support groups are often wonderful places where you can receive positive attention from people. The positive effects have helped millions climb out of negative situations, conditions they might not have been able to overcome on their own. The powerful attention of the support group works in the same way as the Voodoo curse, but instead of destroying—it heals.

Energy

There is one special benefit to this work that will be achieved if you seriously take on a commitment to develop and strengthen your emotional body. As you utilize the emotional cleansers to help purge your body of emotional toxins, and you shift your behavior from chasing toxic desires to seeking healthy goals, your daily energy will increase.

Do you remember, as a child, waking up in the morning and jumping out of bed, filled with energy and enthusiasm, ready to take on the adventures and challenges of the new day? Do you have memories of running and jumping and playing, non-stop, for hours at a time? Do you remember how your body could easily spring into action in a flash? How do you feel, these days, when you wake up in the morning? Do you need one or two cups of coffee before you can "feel" awake? Do you feel tired just thinking about the upcoming day, and of all the things you have to do?

Most people these days don't seem to have the energy, enthusiasm, and endurance they once had. Most people are doing their best to function each day in spite of tremendous feelings of fatigue and exhaustion. There are a number of reasons that this tiredness is affecting so many people. Some obvious reasons have to do with the kinds of laid-back lifestyles some of us have chosen. Indulging in drugs, alcohol, nicotine, caffeine, watching hours of TV, etc., has exhausting effects on our bodies, whether we have chosen these lifestyles with awareness or have just fallen into them. We each have the right to live the way we choose. If you still choose a laid-back kind of lifestyle after reading this book, I wish you well. I, personally, have made the decision to choose a way of life focused more on being "sharp and alert," and will enthusiastically encourage everybody I care about to do the same. I think it's better and more fun to experience life with all eight cylinders working well.

We've learned much more about health and well-being over the past few years, with the movement toward a more conscious life. We've learned that cigarettes, alcohol, and drugs are numbing agents that shut down and/or alter the physical body, and basically permeate the system with toxins. We know these substances are not healthy and the less we indulge in these toxic substances, the less work our bodies will have to do to remain in good shape. We've learned that certain foods like meats and dairy products, as well as large amounts of sugar, put pressure on the body, requiring longer periods for digestion, which can ultimately lead to minor nuisance illnesses in the short-term and major, life-threatening diseases eventually. We've learned that food devoid of preservatives, chemicals, and pesticides is better for the body and will be digested more easily, with far fewer negative side-effects. We've learned about the importance of drinking lots of water on a daily basis to insure regular cleansing of the system. We've learned that regular exercise is essential for the body to sustain its good working condition, and that a sedentary life style is much more apt to be filled with illness and disease. (I have a chiropractor friend who has observed that many of his patients who exercise during periods of illness often heal much more effectively than those patients who take the route of bed-rest.) More often than not, moving the body and breathing in fresh air will help it in its attempt toward homeostasis and balance.

We've learned that stretching and strengthening the muscles will keep the body in a healthy state, and that activities like weight-bearing exercise help sustain good bone density and are deterrents to osteoporosis. We've learned that since the essential nutrients in our food supply have slowly been diminishing, our need to take vitamins and supplements on a regular basis has been increasing.

In spite of all these important developments, however, we still have not mastered the art of reclaiming and sustaining our natural energy on a daily basis. Many of us attempt to "trick" our bodies by pumping them with caffeine and sugar products, but the temporary surge of energy from those items only masks underlying exhaustion.

If you attempt to detox from coffee or caffeine products, you might initially get a throbbing headache that could last from a couple of days to two weeks, followed by a period of lethargy. This is the body's attempt to heal from the effects of those amphetamine-like products. Most people won't attempt to detox from coffee. It's much more difficult than they think, and it certainly will disturb the "normal," hyperactive, up-tempo life style in which so many people find themselves immersed. This kind of life style can be just as unhealthy and exhausting to the body as being overly laid-back.

Sometimes we appear to be like wilting flowers and vines, draped all over each other and strangling each other in an attempt to steal one another's remaining energy. If we can only learn that the energy we attempt to steal away from someone else is a temporary fix and cannot help us reclaim our own life force, then we can rightfully focus on reclaiming our own energy.

The good news is that we can reclaim a good bit, if not all, of our own energy, and that our bodies will jump for joy when we make the decision to go after reclaiming this energy. It's almost like breathing. There's so much air around us, yet most people don't breathe deeply. They breathe just enough to stay alive. There's all the free air in the world, and the more deeply we breathe, the more deeply we feel, the more clear our thoughts become, the better our bodies function, and the more energy we have. Yet, we as a society stay locked into a sub-ventilating type of breathing, which helps sustain our exhausted state. When we temporarily "lose control" and unconsciously slip into a state of deeper breathing, we often get dizzy and falsely identify this state as hyperventilation. This is just deep breathing, although it frequently opens the door to some old, uncomfortable feelings and emotional toxins. Most people don't want to deal with those "hidden skeletons" and will quickly go back to shallow breathing. It is a safer way to live, but is also more stagnant.

One way to begin reclaiming your energy is to start breathing more deeply. When you start this deeper breathing, you then will need to release whatever emotional toxins surface. If you release these toxins and allow your body to come to a natural, more relaxed state with the deep breathing, you will inevitably feel lighter and have more energy.

In general, when we suppress emotional toxins, we put an extra burden on the body's system that eventually leads to some form of physical exhaustion. On the other hand, when we release these emotional toxins, we free the body of unneeded tension, and the result almost always is a surge of energy. Anybody who has ever had a powerful counseling session, when a significant amount of emotional toxins have been released, knows what I'm talking about. When those heavy emotional toxins are released, your body actually feels lighter, as if a weight has been taken off your shoulders. For those who are not consistently releasing these emotional toxins, the heavy feeling that they carry tends to increase and get even heavier as they grow older. Many people have lived so long with that heaviness in their bodies that they don't even realize that anything is wrong. However, carrying that kind of burden takes its toll.

The whole area of aging, as we know it, may need to be reviewed and modified. We're so used to the old scenario that portrays us as getting old, getting sick, and then dying. It has always been based on observing people over the generations who have suppressed their natural healing processes, along with inhibiting the development and strengthening of their emotional bodies. Under those conditions it is a major miracle that we've done as well as we have. Our human bodies are so resilient.

However, the number of people over the past generations who died from heart attacks, strokes, cancers, or complications due to arthritic conditions, all of which may have been largely caused or aggravated by emotional tensions, may have distorted the life span statistics researched by the Census Bureau. Our life spans should increase greatly, on average, in the next twenty to forty years as this additional information about the human body and emotions becomes more widespread.

I believe that instead of aging, getting sick, and dying, we actually "die" in spirit, get emotionally and physically sick, and eventually age. We start to die by experiencing hurts, inhibiting our natural healing process due to our conditioning, and setting up a scenario of rigid, patterned behaviors that make our bodies susceptible and vulnerable to the slow build-up of emotional toxins. Subsequently, we get sick, which is what happens to the body as a result of the weakened immune system, directly caused by this build-up of emotional toxins. Inevitably, we age at a very disturbing, unnatural, and accelerated rate. This does not need to happen. If we follow some of the new health tips we've learned about our physical body, and integrate the new information about our emotional body, we give ourselves the power and opportunity to live longer. There is less reason why we can't reach our eighties, nineties and one hundreds with our bodies flexible and toned, our minds alert and aware, and our hearts still filled with enthusiasm and a joy for life.

PART 3: Toward a Clear Heart

അ അ അ

In the first part of this book, I've exposed the crucial forms of emotional toxins that, when allowed to build up on their own, commonly lead us to disconnection, dissatisfaction, isolation, and lives of frustration. I've also given you a detailed picture in Part Two of an effective path toward healing through emotional cleansing. This process is, in effect, a way of life. It is not like a one-time blockbuster explosion that will immediately free you from all the negativity that you've acquired over your years on this planet. It's also not a course that, once completed, will bring you eternal bliss or a "happily ever after" life. (Just for the record, "happiness" is a feeling, a good feeling, but nevertheless it's just another feeling. Feelings will always come and go, just like clouds in the sky.)

In Part Three, I will show you the possibilities that can occur for you if you choose to follow the path of emotional cleansing. "Clear heart" means that your love is free to flow whenever it feels appropriate. The love experienced by those with a clear heart flows both ways—we are open to give our love and we are open to receive love from others. Those with a clear heart have reclaimed a special sensitivity to life, at times being as vulnerable as a rose, other times as strong as an oak tree. People with clear hearts have the flexibility to function effectively in our society while still being able to delight in the intelligence and magnificence of all life in the world. They can act powerfully and confidently while still having the ability to feel a sense of humility and awe from the experiences that life has to offer. People who have reclaimed a clear heart know that experiences of joy and pain will come and go. They can be at peace with either the flow of warm tears or the spontaneous outburst of hearty belly laughs. Those who have cleansed their hearts are at peace with all the body's wonderful life-sustaining mechanisms, whatever they are and whenever they need to happen—"in summer we sweat, in winter we shiver."

In Part Three, I will reveal in depth some qualities that naturally evolve in people who are on the path toward reclaiming a clear heart. These qualities; courage, commitment, integrity, trust, playfulness, community consciousness, and spirituality have strong tendencies to develop in each of us as we go after our life's dreams and goals.

CHAPTER 1: Courage
~~~

I thought it would be appropriate to start Part Three with an in-depth look at the quality of courage, since the word "courage" is derived from the French word for heart, "coeur." I often think of the Cowardly Lion from the Wizard of Oz when I hear the word courage. He believed that he was a coward because he was in touch with his fear. It's too bad I wasn't around to counsel him so he could have trembled away all his stored-up fears from the past that caused him to believe that he was not courageous. But though the lion didn't have a good counselor, Dorothy, with her innocence, clarity, and love, helped the lion see who he really was, separate from his fears. When danger appeared, he came through, together with the Tin Man and the Scarecrow, as they saved Dorothy from the Wicked Witch.

We are all capable of incredible acts of courage, and as we cleanse our hearts from the stored-up toxins from the past, we naturally evolve into the courageous people that we have the potential to be.

For some of us, as for Stanley in the chapter on trembling,

courage will help us fight for the respect that we deserve from others. It will also move us to stand up for what we believe in—acting on the courage of our convictions.

For a large majority of men in the world, as well as many women, it will be an act of courage to make the decision to follow this path of healing. Our conditioning has confused many of us into believing that we are weak and cowardly if we stay open to our emotions. The truth is if we stay open to our emotional bodies we will not be willing to accept conditions that are not supportive of our health and well-being.

Many men in particular have been consistently stifled in their attempts to open their hearts, showing loved ones how much they really care. Our society has made this difficult for men, but things are slowly changing. Men have an incredible capacity to love and be loved, but at this point it still takes courage to keep their hearts open. It was not that hard for them when they were boys.

I worked with a man named Roy at one men's Workshop. He was a thirty-eight-year-old truck driver, toughened from the conditioning of years of trucking. I encouraged him to go back in his memory to a time when he cared deeply and openly for someone or something. I stood quietly and held his hand, listening with respect as he told his story to a group of fifty men.

"I must have been about ten or eleven. We lived in the country and I used to play down at the swimmin' hole. I was pretty shy around people, but I felt comfortable and at home with all the critters. The swimmin' hole was a great place for me. I spent many days just hangin' out there. I was really into the frogs and tadpoles, watching the tadpoles swim around and listening to the croaking of the bullfrogs.

"One day I caught two tadpoles and put them in a jar with some pond water. I wanted to have them close to me in my room. I brought them home and my mom said I could keep them as long as I took care of them. Everyday I caught little insects and dropped them in the jar along with some pond algae. I changed the water every couple of days also. I watched those tadpoles grow bigger everyday. It was really cool. They were my buddies and I guess I was like their mom or something. I loved the little critters.

"Eventually they started turning into frogs and pretty soon they wanted out of the jar in a bad way. I loved 'em so much that I didn't want to let them go. But I knew they would die if I kept them in the jar. I was sad, but I knew what I had to do. I took the jar and went down to the pond. I opened the jar and, after I told them that they were my best friends and would always be my buddies, I slowly lowered the jar into the water. Without any hesitation, they bolted right out of the jar, and into the water, and began swimming away. I cried a bunch, but I knew I did the right thing. They looked so happy and free. They were where they belonged, doing their thing as frogs do.

"It's a whole lot of years later, but I still go to that pond when I go back home to visit my mom. And it still holds some magic for me. To this day, I just love listening to the sound of bullfrogs croaking on a warm, summer night."

As Roy told his story, his tough exterior slowly disappeared, replaced by a softness, the same sweetness he had when he was eleven years old. By the end of the story, most of the fifty men were in tears. The story was touching, but I think most of the men were crying because they, too, had similar memories of times when they were innocent and open with their caring. Hearing Roy's story about the frogs helped each man get in touch with the innocent parts of himself, parts that might have been numbed out and hidden away for years but still remained intact.

For those men, the workshop environment was a safe haven to open their hearts. Everyone needs safety to explore previously forbidden areas. But, in time and with good guidance, as we get more and more relaxed with our emotional bodies, we naturally gain confidence that they truly are wonderful parts of our humanity. However, as long as the majority of our society remains confused about the power of being emotionally connected, the act of expressing oneself emotionally—being vulnerable and showing an open heart—will remain an act of courage.

CHAPTER 2: Commitment

There is a special power that results from taking on and successfully accomplishing commitments to enhance your life. As you continue to cleanse the toxins from your body, your heart will naturally become stronger with more and more clarity, and your connection to yourself, those you love, and the whole planet will blossom.

The first person each of us needs to make commitments to is ourself. When our hearts are clear, the love we have for ourselves—our minds and our bodies—often moves us toward making reasonable and solidly grounded commitments that we can succeed at. We develop a strong sense of what we can do and what we cannot do, and we may typically challenge ourselves in a way that brings joy and a sense of accomplishment. Succeeding at today's commitments develops an environment for succeeding with future resolutions.

I have recently made a commitment to myself to get more exercise. I thought about what my body enjoyed doing and then went about setting up a flexible schedule for myself. I enjoy going for walks, playing drums, and swimming. I made a commitment to myself to do at least one of these activities everyday. In addition, I got a weight machine to strengthen my muscles and am working out three times a week.

The activities are worthwhile, but the key to success is for me to stay conscious of how I feel about myself before, during and after each activity. Equally important is how I feel about myself when I choose to take a day or two off from my routine. The key here is not about rigid compliance to a routine, but to keep thinking thoughtfully and flexibly about what makes sense each day.

I don't want to give myself too big of a goal, like one hundred laps in the pool, when I know that will be too much of a challenge. But I also don't want to give in to goals that are too easy. Basically, I want to be my own coach, thinking well about my body and cheering myself on toward the goal. Why do we often pay good money to get some stranger to tell us what is best for us? I think, in general, it's terribly invalidating to our thinking and to our connection with our own bodies to give those decisions to another human being. Those who have spent years acquiring knowledge and expertise can help us with useful information, but the decision is ours. I'm convinced that the more we do the emotional cleansing work and the more we grow into that clear heart space, the more our thinking about ourselves will be accurate.

The process for me has been exciting. I look forward to the different exercises, marvel at my body's ability to meet the challenges, notice how great if feels to my body to be breathing deeply and using my muscles, and eventually relish the sense of accomplishment after every workout.

Professional coaches will commonly say that the majority of the challenge for athletes is psychological. The problem is not the workout, it's what goes on in our minds before, during, and after the activity.

There is even more power tapped and unleashed when two people make and successfully act on commitments to each other.

At one of my workshops I called up Bonnie and Ray, a couple who had been married for twenty-five years. I asked them to talk a little about how they met, then to share some good memories and some painful ones over the years they had together. Finally, I asked them to talk about the commitment they had to each other. For about an hour, we all heard their special stories, from their inconspicuous beginning, through to marriage, children, and careers. Ray had become a diabetic and Bonnie had struggled with severe loss of hearing. The stories were a mix of bitter and sweet, but the respect, caring, devotion, and pride they showed for each other had everybody at the workshop in tears. Ray said he would do anything for Bonnie. Bonnie didn't have to say much about her commitment. Her devotion to Ray through his struggles with diabetes was as telling as could be. Toward the end of the hour, they held each other, cried, and shook, while beaming their love and commitment for one another throughout the room. It was clean, direct, powerful, and extremely loving—a beautiful moment in time and a great example of what can happen when two people act successfully in a life-long commitment to each other.

CHAPTER 3: Trust
∾∾∾

Those of us who have chosen the path toward clearing our hearts slowly but surely reclaim a deep sense of trust in our own life as well as a deep trust in general.

Many years ago, when I first joined the counseling profession, I was fascinated by observing some women whom I had been counseling. I had been working with three different women who did not know each other. They came to me on different days, their paths never crossing. Each had her own unique issues that she was dealing with, but, from my counseling point of view, all three needed to cry.

In each case, I had been sure that crying was needed to release the emotional toxins that had built up for them. However, no matter what I did as a counselor, nothing worked.

Although I was just a novice counselor back then, I still took pride in my work, and felt frustrated with my inability to help these women. I was respectful to them, well-informed about their lives, and had a pretty good grasp of counseling techniques. Yet nothing worked.

During this time, I was also working, as a client, on my own issues with another counselor. One session was very intense for me. I got in touch with some painful emotions, remembering all my difficult feelings connected with the time my mother took a job and went off to work. I felt like I had been abandoned by her. I cried for the first time in years. I sobbed heavily for a good part of the session, remembering back then how I pleaded with her to stay, but to no avail.

The person counseling me was relaxed with my crying. She understood the healing process, holding me tenderly while softly encouraging the release of the tears. I sensed the safety and trusted her completely.

During the following week, all three women cried with me in their sessions. All three had great sessions and left in much better spirits than they did from previous sessions.

I came to the conclusion that the releasing of tears for the women had not been just a pure coincidence. I figured that, on some intuitive or psychic level, all three knew that I now could be trusted more than before. Something had shifted in me since I'd cried in my session, and I maybe had become a safer counselor for these women. I never spoke to any of them about this change, but with less work and hardly any use of new techniques, my ability to counsel them effectively had improved.

As we clear out the old toxins we become more and more connected to our own life and we develop an intuitive connection to the pulse of the whole world. Some might call it tapping into the cosmic consciousness. Karl Jung called it the collective unconscious. Some might say it's connecting to our psychic powers. I don't have an accurate explanation of why this happens. However, I have observed that it does happen. The more toxins we release, the more connected we become. The more connected we are, the more others sense our safeness and trust us to help guide them on their path toward healing.

People on the path toward a clear heart slowly develop a loyalty to their bodies, faithfully honoring, respecting, and nurturing them. We become more and more aware of what our bodies need, reclaiming a sensitivity to our bodies while cultivating a deep sense of trust in our life force.

People on the path toward a clear heart develop a deep trust in the healing process; in their ability to think clearly and consciously; in their willingness to listen to, respect and nourish their bodies; and in their tendencies to build strong, meaningful friendships.

CHAPTER 4: Integrity
〰〰〰

When we've worked effectively at cleansing our bodies and minds of toxins, we slowly but surely develop a deep connection to "knowing" what is healthy and what is unhealthy for our lives. Sometimes we know through clarity of thought, sometimes through intuition or gut feeling. The more we cleanse ourselves of toxins, the more we develop this quality of knowing and along with it a deep sense of trust in our connection. We also tend to cultivate an uncompromising adherence to what we believe in, the things that are important to us. The seed of emotional cleansing eventually becomes the flower of integrity.

Years ago I participated in a values clarification training. The key part of it was to understand that many of us function with different sets of values. It doesn't necessarily mean that one set of values is more rational than another. We learned that we didn't have to agree with others' beliefs or comply with their values to respect their right to have different points of view. Likewise, we learned that our values were equally as important as the values of others. Self-respect as well as respect for others is one key quality of integrity.

When I think of integrity, I think of the farmers in years past who would shake hands, agreeing on business deals. Once agreed upon, they would both come through with their part of the bargain. There were no lawyers needed, no written contracts, no insurance coverage. Both farmers would honor the agreement because they had self-respect as well as a high regard for their fellow farmer. The handshake was all that was needed. They both respected each other, acting responsibly on their word.

Responsibility is another key quality of integrity. When we are functioning with clear hearts, we don't just think of our own needs. We take the whole picture into consideration. We function with the ability to respond thoughtfully to each situation. If there's a fire, we feel our fear but call the fire department instead of just running and hiding. If someone is hurt, we give that person our support while making every attempt to get help. Whether things are wonderful or difficult, we function responsibly, thoughtful of the whole picture. This includes thinking thoughtfully of ourselves. Sacrificing our own needs is martyrdom and is not a responsible act indulged in by people with clear hearts.

Honesty is a third quality shared by people with integrity. I remember once shopping in a supermarket with my mother during my teenage years. We had checked out, my mother had paid for the groceries and had received her change. She stopped, looked closely at the coins in her hand, and then pointed out to the cashier that she had been given one penny too much. My mother handed the astonished cashier the penny, smiled, and walked out of the store. At first I thought my mom was nuts, but then eventually realized that she was proud of her values, sticking to them without compromise. She had integrity and would never allow herself to take something that wasn't rightfully hers. It wasn't about the penny, but the principle.

Integrity is strengthened when we are honest with ourselves, no matter what the situation and no matter how painful. People who have cleansed themselves of the toxins having to do with both denial and obsession are able to have honest conversations with their inner voices. The more honest you are with yourself, the more you develop a deep trust of your thinking. This is precious.

Being honest with ourselves moves us to being honest with others, no matter how hard it may be. The people who have cleansed themselves of toxins can be honest with others, but are filled with compassion and open hearts in their honesty, rather than criticism and fear.

Integrity, with the accompanying qualities of honesty, respect, and responsibility, does not appear in any way to be charismatic or flamboyant. However, the lives of people with integrity tend to be satisfying and grounded.

Most people who have chosen the path toward a clear heart slowly let go of the compulsion to seek out irrational situations to feel alive, guiding themselves toward being more consistently open to the magnificent and magical wonders that our planet has to offer.

People who live based on their integrity tend to like themselves, too. They commonly experience an inner radiant glow that is natural and attracts others to them. I believe this is one of the human experiences that many people are seeking.

CHAPTER 5: Play

ᘒᘒᘒ

"Angels can fly because they take themselves lightly."

I used to run "play" workshops every summer for adults only. The people who attended were hoping to reclaim their spontaneous, playful behavior, something which most of them had lost years ago. The distresses that had built up during their lives as adults, along with the image of the serious, hard-working and responsible woman or man, had severely interfered with their ability to relax and play in healthy ways. My job was to establish a tone of lightness for the workshop, provide a safe environment for people who might need to release emotional toxins, give some clear information about the value of play, encourage others to play, and model, to the best of my ability, what it might look like to be rationally playful.

Here's a brief summary of what I learned. In the beginning, most folks had to break through a layer of either shame, humiliation, or embarrassment before being able to loosen up and actually play. Some never did. I learned that underneath many sophisticated, dignified, controlled personalities are silly, goofy, playful people, terrified of being ridiculed or humiliated in front of a group. I learned that, no matter how big and scary-looking a man might appear to be, underneath the intimidating appearance there usually is a mushball, longing to be accepted.

We had access to a pond, and in the afternoons we'd spend one hour playing in the water. This benign activity, along with the safe environment, brought up lots of "stuff" for some people. Maureen, a thirty-five-year-old woman, admitted that she would prefer to counsel on her feelings around play, rather than actually get into the water and attempt to play. She said she was more comfortable in the role of client, where she enjoyed talking about all the distresses that made it hard for her to play. After giving her a chance to talk some more, I firmly but lovingly encouraged her into the water, pointing out to her that, at least for awhile, she might have to face and feel the uncomfortable feelings if she really wanted to get through her struggle. She understood, mustered up her courage, and cautiously approached the water. To her surprise, she was welcomed warmly by four or five others, who were supportive. They all began to play together in the water—including Maureen.

Tamara, a thirty-year-old, told me that she was the eldest child from a large family, and had been forced to take care of her younger siblings. Over the years, she developed a pattern of putting the needs of others ahead of her own, typically called a "caretaking" pattern. Her pattern of feeling responsible for everyone made it impossible for her to relax and have fun in the water. She was a good swimmer and she loved being in the water, but was always watching out for the well-being of the group. Acting like the lifeguard was her pattern in action. As long as she was in caretaking mode, the dignified but isolating position as lifeguard, she didn't have to deal with her underlying fear, quietly wondering if others would ever accept her as a friend and want to play with her. I told her that I would take on the role of lifeguard for awhile and encouraged her to play with others in the water. It was challenging, but seemingly more rewarding for her than being limited to the admirable role of lifeguard.

Those of us who have been doing work toward cleansing our hearts from old toxins have slowly acquired an understanding of play. We've learned that play is crucial for our lives to go well, that play on a regular basis is essential for our health and spiritual well-being.

We've released much of the toxicity that was inhibiting our ability to play. We've also released the toxins that compelled us to attempt play with a heaviness, carrying around old baggage from unhealed wounds.

We've learned to play with a lightheartedness, a sense of compassion and caring, taking everyone, including ourselves, into consideration. We have worked toward cleansing our hearts of the old toxic ways, such as competitive play, with the underlying tension, desperation, and obsession focused so much on winning and losing. Our form of competition can be equally as physically challenging, but with a healthy focus toward developing one another's excellence in specific areas. When people on the path toward clear hearts play together, good feelings arise for all. We develop the ability to play with four-year-olds, forty-four-year-olds or eighty-four-year-olds and be engaged and focused. We are constantly working toward that kind of flexibility and we can sincerely enjoy all our playful interactions.

I have observed that the fear of being shamed, embarrassed, or humiliated has methodically stifled and inhibited adults in their natural ability to play with themselves and with others. I've seen so many people like Maureen and Tamara who've been starving for play in their lives, but have been rigidly forced into appropriate adult-like behavior.

Many adults think of sports or some form of competition or sex when they think of play. In spite of the physical releases provided by both sports and sex, the irrational approach so many people have toward these two forms of play is similar to the earlier emotional toxins discussed in Part 1 of this book. The playful activity becomes the place where the unhealed wounds take over and distort healthy functioning. The behavior is toxic and will usually lead people to more isolated lives.

Those of us who are on the path toward reclaiming our clear hearts slowly develop the ability to feel when we are becoming rigid about play or anything else. Life in this society is filled with tensions, daily stresses, and challenges that, if unattended, can easily develop into chronic fixed patterns of behavior. Even those who have reclaimed most of their clear heart are in no way totally protected from these toxins. However, we are very much in touch with our bodies and subsequently are sensitive enough to quickly feel the onset of tension. We also have slowly acquired the kind of awareness, flexibility, and discipline to be able to interrupt this flow of negativity before it has a chance to settle into our systems. This is a great example of what can happen when we combine a conscious mind with a cleansed heart. Thoughtful, unrigid play creates the juice that lubricates our bodies and nurtures our souls.

I love to play. Playing music, swimming, wrestling, hiking, making up games spontaneously, telling stories, giving massages—these activities are all filled with pleasure for me. I can enjoy myself doing most of those things on my own, but it's usually more fun for me with a partner or a group. I have found that the more I can have fun with myself, the more I'm able to be relaxed and playful with others. My energy encourages and supports a safe environment for others to be relaxed and playful with me. Things will usually go well if two or more people can enter a time for play with this attitude. Everybody involved will enjoy the experience. People who are on the path toward clear hearts work cooperatively with each other, are thoroughly satisfied when the play time ends, and feel good about themselves and each other. This kind of play nurtures friendships.

Good friends usually have four important qualities: the ability to play with each other, the compassion to accept each other for who each is and how far each has come, the ability to openly and without caution express love for each other, and the thoughtfulness and firmness to support each other toward health and away from toxicity.

Play, accept, love and support—PALS—four important qualities of good friendships. Those of us who have cleansed our hearts have developed the ability to implement these qualities toward our own selves as well as with our close friends.

CHAPTER 6: CommunityConsciousness

ονονον

It is inherent in all of us to want our lives and the lives of those we love to go well. Due to confusing conditioning and many unhealed hurts acquired over the years, many of us have lost touch with this inherent quality. As we journey through the process of cleansing our bodies of emotional toxins and freeing ourselves from self-centered attitudes based on survival fears, we spontaneously begin to reclaim the natural desire to see that things around us go well.

As this path is set in motion, we do our best to not mistreat our bodies in any way. We know how precious it is to be alive and we cherish life every day, nurturing our bodies and celebrating the fact that we have a growing awareness of our own lives and life itself. We also do our best to weed out of our lives any people who seem compelled to mistreat us. We understand that their destructive behavior is based on unhealed wounds and misinformation, but we also know that allowing negative behavior to continue is detrimental to both our lives and the lives of those who are acting in toxic ways. We have the power to choose flexibly what action makes sense. We can choose to end the relationship. "May God bless them and keep them far away from us." Or we can opt to do our best to help them out of the toxic behavior.

Our hearts are capable of flowing with the intention of love when we try to interrupt toxic behavior. Initially this can be daunting, but those with clear hearts and connection to their emotional bodies will tremble away their fears while maintaining clear focus.

I attended a workshop many years ago that was led by a deeply compassionate man named Charlie. One evening, Charlie described an incident that took place in his life. The story was important to me at the time and helped me understand the difference between focusing on love or fear.

Charlie went to a restaurant with a couple of friends late one evening while on vacation in a small town in Germany. Toward the end of the meal, he and his friends heard loud noises coming from the kitchen. There were screams and angry shouts, and it sounded like someone was in trouble.

Charlie and his two friends went into the kitchen and found a very irate Polish man wielding a knife and yelling at a closed bathroom door. The owner of the restaurant was in the bathroom, too terrified to come out because the Polish man was threatening to kill him.

Charlie didn't speak Polish but slowly approached the knife-wielding man with an open heart. He informed the man through body language that what he was doing was wrong and that he knew the man really did not want to hurt the other person. Charlie stayed a few feet away from the man and gave him lots of quiet, calming attention. The angry man calmed down a little, enough to allow Charlie's other two friends to open the bathroom door and urge the owner out. They stayed with the owner at the other end of the room while Charlie remained with the Polish man. The whole ordeal took about an hour until order was restored. The restaurant owner and the Polish man did not hug, shake hands, or otherwise indicate having made up. But nobody got hurt, and that was the most important thing at the time.

Charlie said it was one of the longest hours of his life, but he obviously felt good about the results. He said that whenever he looked at the knife in the Polish man's hand he got scared and began trembling. After a few shakes, though, he would spontaneously focus on the man's eyes and a calm would take over his body. He could see in the Polish man's eyes how terrified he was and could sense his desperation and confusion. When Charlie saw the knife, he went right into his own fear, but when he focused on the other man's eyes he felt compassion for this man who was isolated, hurting badly, deeply confused, and terrified.

When Charlie looked into the Polish man's eyes he could feel compassion for the man, but when he saw the knife he could only feel his own terror. Anytime you interrupt another person's toxic behavior, you will come face to face with the same choice. If you focus on the toxicity, you probably will not be successful. However, if you focus on the other person, his struggle and spirit, you will have a greater chance of being effective.

Those who are on the path toward having a clear heart will find themselves feeling more compassion for their families, friends, and neighbors and will naturally want the lives of all to thrive. Wanting their lives to go well and actually doing something about it are two very different things, however. Those of us with a clear heart will often spontaneously embark on a path toward seeing to it that things do go well. Intention. This response tends to come naturally, but it is still an act of power. Each one of us has the ability to assist others in enhancing the quality of their lives. For some this will come easily, but for others it will not. The key here is to remember that when we step out of timidity and boldly assert ourselves in a way that we've never done before, initially we may feel awkward and clumsy and even a little intimidated. This is just another level of emotional cleansing taking place. The more powerfully we act in the world, the more our old powerless feelings will come to the surface to be cleaned out. Those working toward clear hearts understand that they may need to release some tears, some rage, some laughter, or shake some on the way toward achieving their goals. The process of learning and growing is one that lasts a lifetime.

Those of us working toward a clear heart will naturally and spontaneously begin to think in terms of a community consciousness. We will also discover creative ways to implement our individual and unique ideas as we joyfully find methods to enhance our lives and the lives of those around us. Each one of us can make an incredible difference!

In the next few years I am going to do my best to purchase some land and build a center to attract the kind of people I want to have in my community. This center will have an alternative school that will teach children about human relationships from a compassionate point of view. Of course the students will learn reading, writing, and arithmetic, but the focus will be on nurturing the intelligence and gifts of each individual—the true meaning of education. The school will be kindergarten through the twelfth grade so that the children can circumvent the whole public school system, which tends to be filled with competition, unhealthy peer pressure, and rigid ideas of learning.

Parents will be required to participate actively in the school. They'll also be required to attend occasional classes and workshops focused on healthy parenting. No matter what students learn at school, they will still be profoundly influenced by the actions and behavior of their parents. If we are to make important changes in the lives of future generations as well as community members in the present, we need to take the whole picture of family life into consideration. Although some parents may initially see this as an extra burden on their lives, nevertheless, in time they too will benefit greatly from the healing that will inevitably ensue, including their own releasing of emotional toxins.

Separate from the school will be a healing center. It will be scheduled with lectures, classes, and workshops for anybody in the community who wants to learn about health and well-being and deeper, connected human relationships. There may be a massage school or a music school to encourage the understanding of healthy touch as well as to develop a sensitivity and appreciation of creative energy. Hydrotherapy, the use of water in healing, will be available, as well as practice in yoga, Tai Chi, and Qigong. Healthful, fresh vegetarian food will nourish all community members.

The school and its students will frequently be exposed to the classes and workshops that take place at the center. As well, the community members that attend the center will be integrated into the events that take place at the school.

The glue that holds communities of people together is their unwavering commitment toward a common goal, a common interest, and a belief in some higher power—spirituality. This will be the umbrella of energy that oversees the whole community.

Hilary Rodham Clinton wrote about the need for community in her book *It Takes a Village*. I am going to do my best to bring to fruition my creative picture of what that looks like, and I wholeheartedly encourage you to do the same.

CHAPTER 7: Spirituality
ᘯᘯᘯ

I was born into this life as a Jew. Although my father was raised in Germany by a Lutheran woman who celebrated Christmas, I still went to Hebrew school and was barmitzvahed when I turned thirteen. I enjoyed the singing in synagogue and was in awe of the rabbi and his expression of love and pride in his Jewishness, but never really felt connected spiritually through my religion. To this day, I feel proud of my Jewish heritage and consistently attend services on the High Holy Days. But this, although very meaningful to me, does not fill my need for a regular and consistent connection to my spirituality.

Over the years, I unconsciously filled my desire for connection with many visits to the beach and the country. Listening to the roar of the ocean on a stormy day or sitting peacefully in the sun in a quiet meadow in the country filled me with serenity and a connection to the bigger picture. I used to love to bundle up and go out in the middle of winter blizzards just to feel the energy of the storm, or climb to a mountain top to experience the swirling and chaotic winds.

I became a meteorologist, almost as a tribute to my fascination with the weather, its power, and all its glory. This was my connection.

Music and singing also filled me with a sense of joy and gratitude. What a blessing to hear one hundred voices resonating through a huge hall. I still get chills down my spine and am often moved to tears from the sound of beautiful voices in harmony. This is also a deep connection for me.

The earth, the sun, the air we breathe, and the water are sources of fulfillment for me along with the joy I feel for being blessed with life, intelligence, awareness, and healthy, loving intimacy with my friends.

Spirituality can be enjoyed in many ways. There are no rules that apply, from my point of view. There is no right and wrong way of tapping into your connection with spiritual energy. Houses of worship have been successfully used for hundreds of years to accomplish this, but for some people it may be as simple as washing the dishes or quietly knitting on a porch. The key is not how you tap into your spiritual energy, but that you find a way that works for you.

Those on the path toward a clear heart will methodically unravel their layers of distress, permanently healing old wounds with the release of emotional toxins. As these layers disintegrate and fall away like layers of an onion, we naturally move a little closer to our essence. The closer we get to our core, the more in touch we become to our energy as well as the energy around us. Often our logical thinking slowly transcends more toward "intuitively knowing." Our ability to slow down and tap into that deep, peaceful inner calm at our center grows stronger.

Healing, cleansing our hearts, and freeing our minds and bodies from emotional toxins is a spiritual journey. Releasing these poisons leads to a clear heart, which allows a deep connection with our life energy, our own spirits, and the spirit of life itself.

Marty Klein is the founder and president of Southern Springs Holistic Learning Center, residing in Tallahassee, Florida. Southern Springs is a not-for-profit 501(c)3 educational retreat center, founded in November 1998. The mission of Southern Springs is to enrich the lives of people of all backgrounds by providing experiential learning opportunities in the areas of healthy living, self-development, community-building, and the creative arts.

If you have an interest in attending workshops or are seeking more information about Southern Springs, please visit our web site at www.southernsprings.org or call (850) 878-8643.

ᏬᏬᏬ